Obsidians in the Valley of the Volcanoes, Peru

A geoarchaeological analysis

Michał Wasilewski

BAR International Series 2223

2011

Published in 2016 by
BAR Publishing, Oxford

BAR International Series 2223

Obsidians in the Valley of the Volcanoes, Peru

ISBN 9781407307817 paperback

ISBN 9781407337760 e-format

DOI https://doi.org/10.30861/9781407307817

A catalogue record for this book is available from the British Library

BAR Publishing is the trading name of British Archaeological Reports (Oxford) Ltd.
British Archaeological Reports was first incorporated in 1974 to publish the BAR
Series, International and British. In 1992 Hadrian Books Ltd became part of the BAR
group. This volume was originally published by Archaeopress in conjunction with
British Archaeological Reports (Oxford) Ltd / Hadrian Books Ltd, the Series principal
publisher, in 2011. This present volume is published by BAR Publishing, 2016.

BAR
PUBLISHING

BAR titles are available from:

BAR Publishing
122 Banbury Rd, Oxford, OX2 7BP, UK
EMAIL info@barpublishing.com
PHONE +44 (0)1865 310431
FAX +44 (0)1865 316916
www.barpublishing.com

For my parents-in-law

Contents

1. INTRODUCTION

1.1. Location and geographical characteristics of the Valley of the Volcanoes

In the southern part of the Republic of Peru, in the Arequipa Departament, there extends the little-known until recently Valle de los Volcanes, or the Valley of the Volcanoes (Fig. 1). It is around 65 km long and is located between a latitude of 15°05' and 15°41' S. It thus extends in a nearly southerly direction (along 72°20' W), between the massifs of Nevado Coropuna (6425 m above sea-level (a.s.l.)) to the west, and Cordillera Shila (around 5600 m a.s.l.) to the east, and drops from the edge of Altiplano (4900–5100 m a.s.l.) in the north, to the Colca River Canyon (around 1350 m a.s.l.) in the south. Administratively, the Valley of the Volcanoes currently lies in the territories of two Peruvian provinces. The larger part belongs to the Castilla Province, while a small area of *puna* to the north-west of the municipality of Umachulco, situated in the upper part of the valley, is found in the Condesuyos Province (Cayarani District). There are five districts – the smallest administrative units – in the territory of the valley: Ayo, Chachas, Andahua, Chilcaymarca and Orcopampa.

The Valley of the Volcanoes is around 360 km away from the department capital, Arequipa, which is Peru's second largest city. The very difficult conditions of the terrain, however, meant that it was in fact cut off from the remaining parts of its home department until the second half of the 20th century A.D. While it is true that, at least since the times of the Incas, the Valley (and particularly the region of the present town of Orcopampa) has been known for its deposits of gold, it was only possible to reach it on foot or by horse from the northern side (i.e. from Cusco). This corner, isolated from the rest of the world, gained road access only in the 1980s, precisely due to the development of gold-mining. The activities of the Peruvian Buenaventura Mining Company (Compañía de Minas Buenaventura) brought about the expansion of the Valley's infrastructure in a particular way. The enterprise not only built a network of roads, but also led to the establishment of high-tension power lines, a series of local hydro-electric plants, telephone and internet connections and greater hydraulic foundations, not to mention school buildings and basic health service (1 hospital in Orcopampa; besides that there exists an independent *Centro de Salud*, or medical clinic in Andahua). Despite these investments, the valley remains quite poor. Roads as a rule (aside from small segments in cities) have only a hardened surface. Electricity in most municipalities comes from local hydroelectric power stations (recently, solar batteries have also appeared), but a large part of smaller settlements lack it completely. Only a few larger towns have small waterworks, while there is a universal lack of sewage systems. In the vicinity of Orcopampa there is a landing field for light aircraft, which is basically used only for the needs of the mine.

In the central part of the Valley of the Volcanoes lies the town of Andahua (3550 m a.s.l.) – the seat of local government and informal capital of the valley. The municipality situated below is Ayo (1800 m a.s.l.), and above it – the mining town of Orcopampa (3900 m a.s.l.) and a settlement with thermal springs, Huancarama (3950 m a.s.l.). Second-

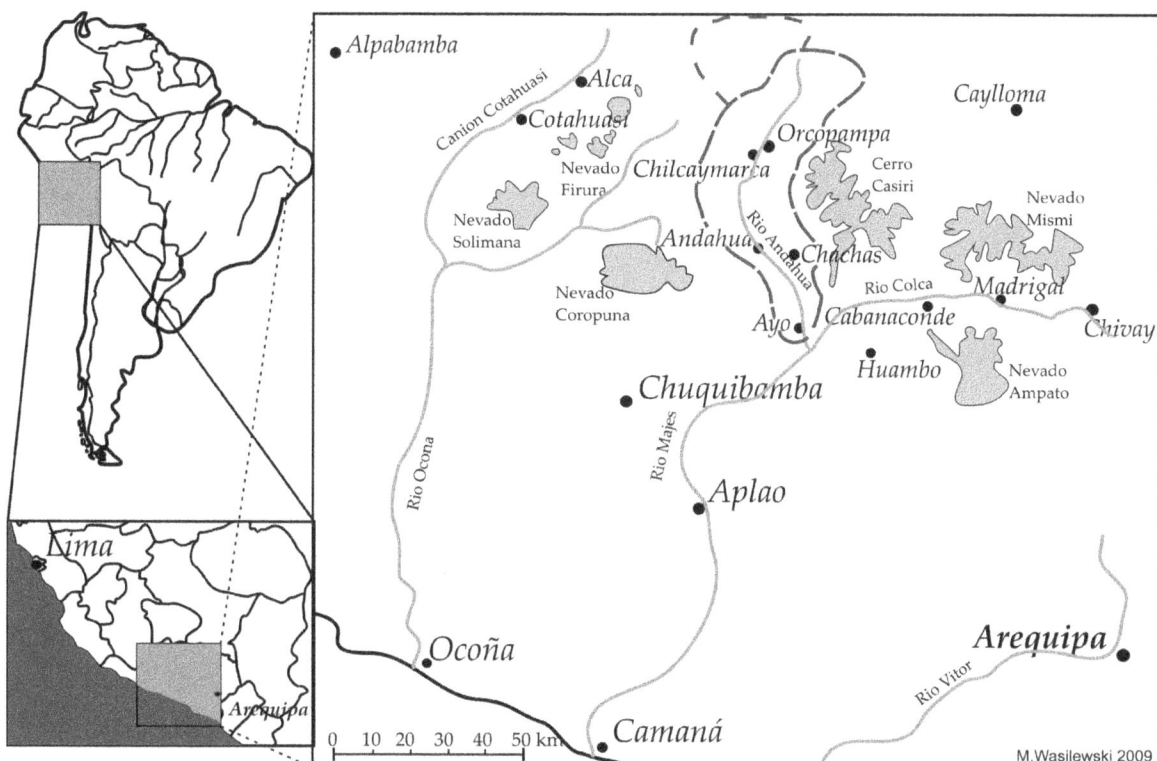

Fig. 1   Map representing the location of the Valley of the Volcanoes (the solid line) and Pampa Jararanca (the broken line)

ary and tertiary municipalities are Chachas, Chapacoco, Chilcaymarca, Misahuanca, Umachulco and Arcata. Besides this, Sucna, Sarpane, Palcacha and Panahua are worth mentioning. One must also remember that across the entire valley, on its slopes and the puna surrounding it, there is a series of dispersed settlement points numbering from 1–5 homes, often occupied temporarily. The population of the largest municipalities is estimated to be: for Orcopampa, around 4500 (including a large percent of migrant residents – miners), and for Andahua 1500–2000. In total, the Valley of the Volcanoes is settled by 15000–16000 residents. The figure given encompasses also migrant labor, which can be as much as 45% of the present population. The remaining part of the population is mainly farmers and herders of Metis origin and to a lesser extent Indian. Judging from field observations, the level of illiteracy may be as high as 20%; the illiterate are mainly women between the ages of 30–60 years, and men over 40. The dominant language in the area of the valley is Castilian (*castillano*), and the second most commonly known and used language is one of the *Quechua* dialects. Here it should be noted that a small percent of residents (basically, only women from more remote settlements) speak only the *Quechua* language. This is caused both by the still limited contact with the outside world and by the low level of education in the territory of the valley. This phenomenon is, after all, widespread in mountainous parts of Peru and other countries of the Andes. The religion that dominates nowadays is eclectic Catholicism, with distinct pre-Christian elements. Recently, however, a growth in the number of Protestant communities has been observed, and even the appearance of so-called new religious movements (for example, those connected with New Age or Buddhism). The average life expectancy of residents is estimated to be around 50 years.

As already mentioned, the basis of the population's subsistence is mining, herding and agriculture. The service sector is weakly developed and represented in larger municipalities mainly through retail trade, the hotel-restaurant industry, telecommunications and transportation services. There is also one construction-roadwork company in the valley, and a small fraction of residents work in state administration, the police, health and education services. Raising trout, which was introduced to this area, is gaining ever greater significance. Most economic activity, besides agriculture and animal husbandry, is generated by the presence of the mining company. In recent years, a small tourist movement has begun to appear, but does not bring the residents substantial income.

In the surroundings of the Valley of the Volcanoes, there rise several large, known stratovolcanoes (Nevado Coropuna, Nevado Firura, Cerro Cajchaya, Cerro Chinchón; Fig. 94). The Valle de los Volcanes itself, like many other valleys of the Andes, passes through a series of elevation-climatic zones. They vary in their microclimates (amount of precipitation, average temperatures, etc.), and consequently in their cover of plant and animal life (for example, Aldenderfer 1998). The lowest level is the so-called *quechua*, or in the quechua language, "land of temperate climate." It extends from between 2300–3500 m a.s.l.. The second zone, between 3500–4000 m a.s.l., is the *suni*

(quechua: "high, vast"), and finally the highest of those that interest us – the *puna* (4000–4800 m a.s.l.), also called the *soroche*, in reference to the local name for the altitude sickness that is widespread there. In the *quechua*, agriculture and animal husbandry dominate, the *suni* is characterized by the decreasing amount of cultivation and growing significance of llamas and alpacas with increasing altitude. The *soroche* is a terrain on which almost exclusively camelids (today, sheep as well) are raised.

Just as in the entire equatorial-tropical zone, the year is divided into the dry season ("winter," *austral winter*), lasting from May until September, and the rainy season ("summer," *austral summer*), which lasts from October until April. The average temperatures in the "winter" are 9–25°C during the day, and –10 – –3°C at night. In the "summer," they are, respectively, 12–27°C and –3–4°C. Obviously with increasing absolute altitude, the average temperatures for day and night decrease. During the dry season, there is almost no precipitation (10–50 mm), and the cloud-cover is small or absent. However the rainy season is characterized by intensive precipitation (100–180 mm) and a frequent, large cloud-cover. Due to the latitude, the day lasts from 6:00–18:00 in the "winter," while in the "summer" it is a bit longer – 5:00–19:00. In the valley there are winds present throughout the whole year, sometimes quite strong and gusting, and essentially only nights are windless, but cold. These conditions cause a risk of rapid heat loss in living organisms. During the day, winds blow along the axis of the main valley and the axis of its branches. Their greatest intensity occurs in the morning hours (most often towards the bottom of the valley, so-called down-slope winds) and in the afternoon (towards the top of the valley).

The valley's drainage basin consists of tens of small waterways, brooks and streams than join into creeks and rivers, some of which are of an intermittent nature. Most of them begin in the *puna* zone, from springs or vast, flat wetlands. Some of them also originate in the melting zone of mountains glaciers. In this highest level of the valley there are also a dozen or so lakes.

Most streams flowing from the *puna* have the character of mountains streams and thus have a high erosion potential. In the axis part of the Valley of the Volcanoes, the waters join to form a river that is initially called Huaucarama[1], then Orcopampa and finally Andahua. Just as the valley itself, this river joins with the Rio Colca and flows to the Pacific Ocean under the name Rio Majes. The main river mentioned in the Valley of the Volcanoes has the character of a mountain river with high erosion potential, only over the Chilcaimarca-Lomas Pinculluna segment (around 10 km in the upper part of the valley) is it a river with low erosion potential. In its lower segment, below the municipality of Chachas, the river creates an extensive lake, Laguna de Chachas (Fig. 2). In the dry season, the lake has a smaller surface area, and the river disappears immediately below it. In the rainy season, the expanse of water is vaster, and the river is still visible on the surface for around 2 km. The subterranean segment of the Rio Andahua thus extends from 16–20 km, after which the waters appear on the surface 1000 m below, from the spring at the elevation of the Ayo municipality, and falls into the next lake, Laguna Mama-

Fig. 2. Laguna de Chachas – the broads of the Rio Andahua in the winter season, on the right cultivated terraces of the Chachas municipality are visible (phot. M. Wasilewski)

cocha[2], from which it flows through a deeply-cut, 5-kilometer canyon to the Rio Colca.

Among the several tens of tributaries of the main river in the Valley of the Volcanoes, the largest and most important are (in orographic order): Huayta-Pisaca-Quenco, Utjo-Cochasique-Misapuajio-Chilcaimarca, Acalcane-Jararanca-Umachulco-Chilcaimarca, Sora-Auchaca-Ocoruro, Ancasi-Palcuyo-Ocoruro, Tauca, Puncuhuayco-Arhuaya, Ayaniri, Collpa-Ayo. Below the Chachas municipality, all waterways flowing down the valley slopes disappear into ponors.

The Valley of the Volcanoes has a differentiated morphology. With regards to Colca Canyon, it is a hanging valley (Fig. 3). Its slopes either have the character of rocky walls, or are unusually steep and difficult to access, while the bottom – formed from fresh lavas in the lower part of the valley – has a very sharp relief and is difficult to cross, has mostly a sparse covering of vegetation, is dry and uninhabited. The relative altitude of the valley's slopes varies between 500–1000 m on the eastern side, and 800–1200 m on the western side. Such amplitudes appear, as a rule, in a 1–2 km segment (Fig. 4). Both the slopes of the main valley and the floor covered with three generations of lava streams, volcanic cones and gravels maintain their character up until Lomas Pinculluna at 3/4 the of the valley's length (Fig. 5). Higher than 3000 m a.s.l., where older lava formations begin to dominate, greater vegetation, settlement and cultivated terrain already appear on the somewhat eroded, smoothed out relief (Fig. 6). Only above the level area men-

tioned (Lomas Pinculluna) does the floor, covered with fluvial deposits, become easily accessible, and the slopes have a somewhat smaller gradient (Fig. 7). The morphology thus sketched is enriched by canyons. They are formed in three regions. The first, most highly situated of these are the canyons in the upper reaches of the rivers flowing from the *altiplano* (it is enough to mention Utjo-Cochasique-Misapuajio, or Acalcane-Jararanca-Umachulco) (Fig. 8a). The second, equally picturesque area with canyons is formed by the Andahua River on a segment of Pampa Colao Colo-Laguna de Chachas (in places even flowing underground and appearing on the surface in the form of high waterfalls) (Fig. 8b, c). The last, already mentioned fragment of the Andahua River (sometimes called Rio Mamacocha in this segment) also cuts deep into the valley bottom. Between the fresh lava stream and the valley wall formed from carbonate rock, it creates a 5-kilometer canyon, the depth of which reaches 1100 m in places (Fig. 4).

The first (and only, in the lower part of the valley) settlement (Ayo) is located, like most of the others, along the orographically right side of the Valle de los Volcanes, at the opening of a side valley that is shaped differently than the main one. The former is a typical, U-shaped valley, which also has less steep and lower slopes, and the floor is lined with river, slope and glacial sediments. As already mentioned, most of the large side valleys and municipalities are located on the orographicaly right side of the Valley of the Volcanoes. Exceptions to this rule are the Puncuhuayco-

Fig. 3. The union of the Rio Andahua and the Ria Colca. On the left side, above the Rio Colca, the floor of the Valley of the Volcanoes is visible (phot. M. Wasilewski)

Arhuaya and Ayaniri Valleys and the municipality of Chachas (Fig. 9), as well as the group of valleys and municipality of Panahua (known for its picturesque icefalls). Above them, on the eastern side, is situated a vast, highly raised caldera, in the surroundings of which metallic mineralization developed, one of the bases of the earlier-mentioned gold mining. Due to this shape, the Valley of the Volcanoes is a lot easier to access from the western side, where today, as well, the main transportation connections are found (for a long time, it was easier to get here from the direction of Cusco than from Arequipa). The second possibility for reaching it is the trail leading from Colca Valley (from the municipality of Chivay and Caylloma), circling round the caldera mentioned from the north. It is shorter and recently has become increasingly popular thanks to the development of tourism in the region of Chivay. There are plans to build a foot bridge over Colca Canyon, not far from its connection with the Valle de los Volcanes.

The entire Valley of the Volcanoes rises rather steeply to the top from the level of 1800 m a.s.l. at the connection with Colca Canyon, to nearly 4000 m a.s.l. in its highest parts. Above the municipality of Orcopampa the cone and lava streams of the Cerro Antapuna volcano prevail. By way

Fig. 4. Steep slopes, rock walls rising above the end segment of the Rio Andahua (phot. M. Wasilewski)

Fig. 5.   Difficult-to-access floor of the Valley of the Volcanoes, around 5–7 km below the municipality of Andahua (phot. M. Wasilewski)

Fig. 6.   Cultivated terraces in the immediate vicinity of the municipality of Andahua (phot. M. Wasilewski)

Fig. 7. Gentle slopes and the flat floor of the valley seen from above the municipality of Chilcaymarca (phot. M. Wasilewski)

of the many branches of the Valley of the Volcanoes, in its middle and upper parts, it is possible to reach a vast plateau, located in the *puna* zone (Fig. 10). These flat geomorphological formations with abundant lakes and wetlands (Fig. 11), are commonly used today as pasture land for llamas and alpacas, and in the past it was also one of the main biotopes settled by hunter-gatherers and pastoral people.

Contrary to appearances, the vegetation cover of the Valley of the Volcanoes is fairly rich. In the lower parts, like in other terrains of the Andes below 3500 m a.s.l., there appear numerous species that favor a warm, dry habitat, among which there are mainly succulent plants: *Weberbauecerus weberbaueri* (one of the species of columnar cactus, Fig. 12), *Arequipa erectocylindrica* (a small, round cactus), *Corryocactus puquiensis* (sancayo, a cactus with edible fruits), *Tephrocactus barteri* (= *Cumulopuntia sphaerica*, Fig. 13). Among other plants, it is worth mentioning the representatives of the geranium family (*Geraniaceae*): *Balbisia weberbaueri*; aster family (*Asteraceae*): ambrosia shrub (*Ambrosia fruticosa*), *Encelia canescens*, *Diplostephium tacorense* and *Grindelia montana* (*Chiri chiri*); mallow family (*Malvaceae*): *Tarasa operculata* and the legume family (*Fabaceae*): *Adesmia spinosissima*. Dry-habitat bushes are also known, for example Andean ephedra (*Ephedra americana* or *andina*, also called *pinco-pinco*, a trailing bush from the bare-stem, broad-leaf subclass). In the rainy season, one can find numerous, annual grasses (true grasses – *Gramineae*). Both in this zone and in the next, the fique plant, or agape (*Furcraea andina*), is commonly found (for example, Pearsall 1980).

In the *suni* zone, plants are grouped into two biotopes – the so-called dry pampa (*pampa seca*) and clusters of mountain thickets.[3] The most characteristic vegetation of the *pampa seca* includes the stipa (*Stipa ichu*, *Stipa obtusa* (*tisña*), dry-habitat, spiny grasses, called *ichu*[4] by the local people, Fig. 14) and the related bunchgrass (*Festuca orthophylla*, called *coirones*, *iro ichu* or *paja de puna*). Other herbaceous plants of this zone are the plantagos (for example *Plantago monticola*, or *P. linearis*). There also appears a series of different species of small shrubs, like the milk-vetch (*Astragalus garbancillo*, called *garbancillo*, a representative of the legume subfamily), or *Margyricarpus pinnatus* (*perla*) and *Tetraglochin alatum* (= *T. strictum*, *canlle*, both are from the *Rosaceae* family, and have small soil-water requirements) and finally many species of cacti of the genus *Opuntia* (called *waraqo*). Dry, mountain thickets are created mainly by shrubs and vines of the order Asterales (*Asterales*): *Braccharis odorata* (*chilca a bidens*), *Parastrephia* sp., *Mutisia acuminata* (*chinchilcoma*, Fig. 15), Andean bidens (*Bidens andicola*, called *quico* or more often *chilca*, or *amor seco*; an annual plant also from the order Asterales). Among them, there can also be found cantuta (*Cantua buxifolia*, locally called *cantuta*, a plant from the Polemoniaceae Order, resembling buxus), buddleja (*Buddleja incana*, called *quisoar blanco*, a shrub from the buddleja family, Order Scrophulariales) and redstem filaree (*Erodium cicutarium*, or *alfilerillo*, a small, green plant with attractive, reddish flowers). Somewhat higher, around 4000 m a.s.l., other representatives of the Order Asterales and the sunflower family begin to appear: *Parastrephia quadrangu-*

Fig. 8.   a) the initial segment of the canyon in the upper course of the Jararanca River; **b**) waterfalls on the Andahua River between Chachas and Andahua; **c**) fragment of the canyon in the middle course of the Rio Andahua (phot. M. Wasilewski)

Fig. 9. The openings of the Puncuhuayco-Arhuaya and Ayaniri Valleys and cultivated terraces near the Chachas municipality (phot. M. Wasilewski)

Fig. 10. The *puna* region below the Poracota Mine (phot. M. Wasilewski)

Fig. 11. The lake and wetlands in the *puna* zone above Colca Valley (phot. A. Świerzowska)

Fig. 12. Llamas eating fruits and new growth of columnar cactus (phot. M. Wasilewski)

Fig. 13. Flowering *Tephrocactus barteri*, also known as *Cumulopuntia sphaerica*, spreads when its barbs catch on passing animals (phot. M. Wasilewski)

Fig. 14. Stipa (*Stipa ichu*) – a dry-habitat, spiny grass, called *ichu* by local people, most often grows in characteristic clusters (phot. M. Wasilewski)

Fig. 15. Andean bidens (*Bidens andicola*, called *chilca* or *amor seco*) an annual plant from the Order Asterales, it has substantiated medicinal renown (phot. M. Wasilewski)

Fig. 16. A very widespread shrub in the high Andes, *Parastrephia quadrangulare*, called *tola* by the locals (phot. M. Wasilewski)

lare (*tola*, shrub, Fig. 16), *Senecio nutans* (*chacha kume*, or old man; a small, annual plant related to tussilago and arnica), *Baccharis emarginata* (*jinch'umallant'a* or *carqueja*, a shrub-like plant), and also *Atriplex atacamensis* (saltbush, order caryophyllales, a plant related to the beet and amaranth), *Opuntia floccosa* (growing at high altitudes, frost-resistant huaraco, which forms low, wide, pillow-like clusters, covered with the fine hairs of its needles, Fig. 17) and several other species that better tolerate cold climatic conditions.

In the highest plant communities, there still appear stipa grasses (*Stipa* sp.) and festuca (*Festuca* sp.), as well as the asterales (*Parastrephia* sp., *Baccharis* sp.) and *Tertaglochin alatum*. Among other species known are bromus (*Bromus lanatus*, *shockla*, a dry-climate grass), other Asterales from the genera *Werneria* sp. (*pupusa*) and *Perezia* sp. (*sutuma* or *escorzonera*), as well as many *Caryophyllaceae*: *Arenaria lanuginosa* (spreading sandwort, one of the few

shrubs belonging to the Order Caryophyllales), *Paronychia andina* (*gateadora*, a syzygium with creeping stalks that grow in clusters), *Pycnophyllum molle* and *P. bryoides* (*pesque-pesque*). In wet and boggy terrains in the *puna* zone, ecologically important species are encountered: *Distichia muscoides* (*kunkuna*, or *champa*), woodrush *Luzula peruviana* (a small grass from the rush family, *Juncaceae*), ryegrass *Lolium* sp. (a grass from the *Gramineae* family), representatives of the *Alchemilla* genus (*Alchemilla pinnata*, *sillu-sillu* and *A. diplophylla*, *libro-libro*, perennials from the *Rosaceae* family) and several species of reedgrass from the genus *Calamagrostis* (the so-called *crespillo*) (Fig. 18), which is an important component of the diet of Andean camelids (Pearsall 1980).

Higher than 4500 or even 5000 m a.s.l., the *yaretal* plant community is described, in which there live organisms resistant to very low temperatures with a large fluctuation between daytime and nighttime (mosses, lichens, perennials and grasses). For example, it is worth mentioning three species from the genus *Azorella*: *A. yarita* (the so-called *la yareta*), *A. compacta* and *A. diapensoides*. These are plants of economical and medicinal value from the Order *Aralia-*

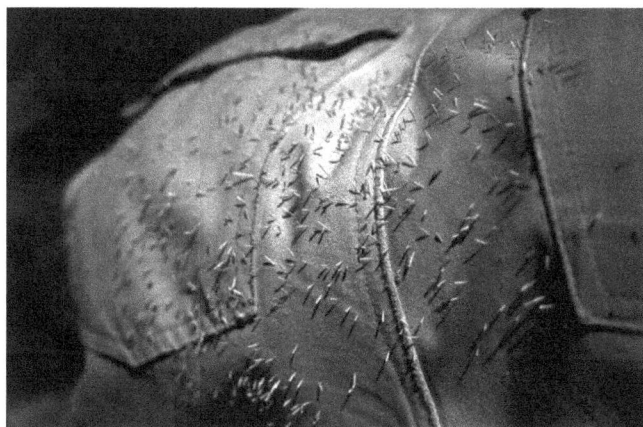

Fig. 17. A frost-resistant cactus (*Opuntia floccosa*) grows at high altitudes in the form of low, wide, pillow-like clusters that look like something one could sit down on to rest, but are covered with many fine needles (phot. M. Wasilewski)

Fig. 18. Small and inconspicuous grasses from the genus of reedgrasses (*Calamagrostis*, the so-called *crespillo*) are an important component of the diet of Andean camelids (phot. M. Wasilewski)

les, which grow on rocks in the form of round, hard caps that reach a height of up to 1 m (Fig. 19). Grasses from the genera *Poa* sp. and *Festuca* sp. also grow there.

Forests, today small and few, although formerly more extensive, consist mainly of the trees *Polylepis incana* (also called *P. besseri* or *P. tarapacana*), that is *queñoa*. They are occasionally accompanied by the mountain cypress (*Austrocedrus chilensis*). They are, after all, dispersed throughout all the altitude-climatic zones starting at 3500 m a.s.l., and are accompanied by different species of shrubs and grasses (Romaña *et al.* 1988, Żurowska 2001).

From among several tens of species of animals living along the entire length of the Valley of the Volcanoes, the most important, although today at times very rare already, are the Andean bear, also called the Peruvian or spectacled bear (*Tremarctos ornatus*), the white-tailed deer, also called

Fig. 19. *Azorella* sp. – a plant of economic and medicinal value, from the Order *Araliales*, grows on rocks in the form of round, hard caps, which reach a height of up to 1 m (phot. M. Wasilewski)

Fig. 20. The plains viscacha (*Lagostomus maximus*) is a rodent just as shy as the European marmot and occupies similar habitats (phot. M. Wasilewski)

the Virginia deer (*Odocoileus virginianus*), the taruca (Hippocamelus antisensis, a mammal from the deer family (*Cervidae*), the vicugna (*Vicugna vicugna*) and the guanaco (Lama guanicoe), puma (cougar, *Puma concolor*), the Andean mountain cat (*Oreailurus jacobita*), colocolo, that is, the pampas cat (*Oncifelis colocolo*), the culpeo or Andean fox (*Dusicyon culpaeus*, a dog-like animal that resembles a jackal), Molina's hog-nosed skunk (*Conepatus chinga, C. rex*, an animal from the mustelidae family resembling a skunk), the plains viscacha (*Lagostomus maximus*, a rodent resembling the chinchilla, but significantly larger than it, Fig. 20), the small chinchilla (*Chinchilla lanigera*), the Bolivian grass mouse (*Akodon boliviensis*), the Andean leaf-eared mouse (*Phyllotis pictus*), the rice rat (*Orizomys* sp., a mouse-like rodent), the guinea pig (*Cavia tschudii, C. aparea*), the mouse opossum (*Marmosa elegans*, the smallest representative of the didelphidae family, the size of a field mouse, often called in Peru raposas, or vixen), the common opossum (*Didelphis marsupialis*) and bats from the vesper family (*Vespertilionidae*): atacama myotis (*Myotis atacamensis*) and Histiotus montanus (Balaguer 1995, Kaulicke 1999, Zwierzęta ... 2005). Amphibians are also encountered, for example frogs from the genus *Telmatobius* (*Telmatobius* sp., *T. rimac*) and Pleurodema (*Pleuro-*

dema marmorata), the arequipensis and Andean toads (*Bufo arequipenis* and *B. spinulosus*) as well as reptiles (for example, lizards from the genera: *Liolaemus* sp., *Stenocercus* sp., *Proctoporus* sp.). Fish are the least numerous group. Only catfish (the so-called bagre, *Trichomycterus* sp. and *Pigydium* sp.) and pupfish (the so-called chalgua, *Orestias* sp.) live here. Nowadays, the rainbow trout (*Oncorhynchus mykiss*) that was introduced here is being raised with increasing intensity. The invertebrate fauna mainly consists of cockroaches, beetles, spiders, ants, etc.

A very large variety of birds are represented here (117 species from 76 genera). The largest and best-known of their representatives are the Andean condors (*Vultur gryphus*, Fig. 21) and the turkey vulture (Cathartes aura). Besides these, this Andean valley is also inhabited by red-backed hawks and puna hawks (*Buteo polyosoma* and *Buteo poecilochrous*; Fig. 22) which live on the slopes and rocks, dry thickets and the puna. The mountain caracara (*Phalcoboenus megalopterus*) is very common. The Andean and Chilean flamingos (*Phoenicoparrus andinus* and *Ph. chilensis*; Fig. 23) feed on the lakes, as do various species of ducks (for example, the puna teal – *Anas puna*, the crested duck – Anas specularioides), coots (the giant coot – *Fulica gigantea*, the American coot – *Fulica americana*)

Fig. 21. Andean condor (*Vultur gryphus*) nesting in Colca Valley, where it is one of the main tourist attractions (phot. M. Wasilewski)

Fig. 23. The tri-colored Andean flamingo (*Phoenicoparrus andinus*) is considered to be the prototype of the Peruvian national flag in terms of its red-white-read coloring (phot. M. Wasilewski)

Fig. 22. Even species of small predatory birds are interested in every potential occasion to feast. This photo shows a puna hawk (*Buteo poecilochrous*) (phot. M. Wasilewski)

Fig. 24. Passerines are an inseparable element of the landscape, not only in the dry *puna* zones (phot. M. Wasilewski)

and representatives of the *Charadriiformes* order, while on the rivers silvery grebes (*Podiceps occipitalis*) are found. On the dry steppe of the *puna* live the ornate tinamou (*Nothoprocta ornata*), the gray-breasted seedsnipe (*Thinocorus orbignyianus*) and several tens of species of passerines (*Passeriformes*; Fig. 24), for example, from the genera *Muscisaxicola* sp., *Carduelis* sp., *Sicalis* sp. and *Phrygilus* sp. Also on dry territories at high elevation, as well as in agricultural areas, the largest species of hummingbird can be encountered – the giant hummingbird (*Patagona gigas*) (Romaña *et al.* 1988).

One should keep in mind the fact that, in the past, the profile of flora and fauna differed somewhat from that of today. Above all, the population of some animals was greater in the past than today. This concerns, in particular, large vertebrates, and among plants – the Chilean cedar (*Austrocedrus chilensis*) which the Spanish exterminated. From among the extinct (or endangered) species found in the higher regions of the Andes, it is worth mentioning: the paleolama (*Palaeolama mirafica*), the Andean horse (*Equus (Amerihippus) andinum*), the American mastodon (*Mammut americanum*), the "long llama" *Macrauchenia* sp.[5], a genus of armadillo (*Eutatus* sp.), deer (for example *Odocoileus virginianus*, *Mazama* sp., *Pudu* sp.), the mountain tapir (*Tapirus pinchaque*) (Deza Rivasplata 1991, Bruhns 1996), and also a large, flightless bird, Darwin's rhea, known as the *suri* or *ñandú andino* (*Pterocnemia pennata garleppi*, also known by the name *Rhea americana*) (Neira Avendaño 1998, Lavallée 2000). Some of these are counted among the so-called megafauna and their extinction is connected not only with climate changes in the period of 11000–8000 B.P. (around 11 050–7050 cal B.C.[6]), but also with the appearance of a new predator and hunter: *Homo sapiens* (for example, Fagan 2004). Another important consequence of the climatic fluctuations was the changes in the elevation reach of particular biotopes. This obviously brought about modifications in their exploitation and the density of the settlement networks in particular zones (for example, Lavallée 1985, Aldenderfer 1998).

Fig. 25. A young fault intersecting the Andahua lava formation and subordinate formations localized in the lower part of the Valley of the Volcanoes (phot. A. Gałaś)

1.2. Geology of the Valley of the Volcanoes

The Valley of the Volcanoes is one of the geologically more interesting, and at the same time less studied regions of the southern part of Peru. It cuts deeply into Mesozoic sedimentary rock, while its floor and slopes are formed by fresh lava and other rocks of the Andahua volcanic formation and – in its upper part – somewhat older volcanic rock, which is connected with metalogenic mineralization (among others, gold-bearing rock).

The entire valley most likely lies on a large fault from the late Mesozoic era. It was also active in later periods, up to the present day, proof of which is the recent (in a geological sense) movement of the intersecting Tertiary and Quaternary lavas and other volcanic rock, visible in the lower part of the valley (the area from the mouth of the Andahua River to Colca; Figs 3, 4, 25). Originally, just as the nearby valleys of Cotahuasi and Colca, the Valley of the Volcanoes surely cut deeply into the Mesozoic sedimentary rock.

The slopes of the Valley of the Volcanoes, almost to the elevation of the Chilcaymarca municipality, are formed from sandstone, slate and limestone from the Jurassic and Cretaceous periods (the so-called Socosani and Yura group). These rocks are strongly folded and cut by faults (Fig. 26), creating high and steep cliff faces. This formation is covered with Neogene formations of the so-called Tacaza Group. It is created mainly by Mesozoic rocks, tuffs, and also lava streams, agglomerate rock and volcanic breccias,

ignimbrite and interstratified sedimentary rock (mainly limnic). The general character of these rocks is defined as andesitic-dacitic (Paulo 2008). In the lower half of the valley, these sediments appear in the form of intermittent coverings, visible in the upper parts of the geological profile. However, above the Chilcaymarca municipality they become the dominant formation on the surface and are the reason for the gentler morphology of the valley slopes (Figs 7, 27). In precisely these formations, more or less siliceous veins are formed, from which chalcedony was later obtained for making tools (see the Appendices).

On the eastern side of the valley, rocks of the Tacaza Group (also called Orcopampa Group locally) form a thick layer covering the complex of mountain chains extending from Cerro Chinchón to Cerro Cerani, or the so-called Cordillera Shilla. In the last stages of their formation, they were enriched with lava domes, volcanic stocks and rhyolite and/or dacite extrusions. Such a turn of events is the reason for the metallic mineralization that this zone is so rich in, forming the basis for the development of gold mining[7] in the valley (the Orcopampa, Layo, Shila and Paula mines). Similar zones of mineralization have been described on the opposite, north-western side of the Valley of the Volcanoes, where sub-surface gold mines are also located (Chipmo, Umachulco, Poracota) (Caldas 1993, Paulo 2008).

Several locally formed units rest on the formations of the Tacaza Group (for example, the Palca, Sillapaca, Ichucollo and Alpabamba Groups), made primarily of vol-

Fig. 26. Rocks of the Yura group, folded and cut by faults, easily visible in the surroundings of the Ayo municipality (phot. M. Wasilewski)

Fig. 27. A view from the bridge in Chilcaymarca overlooking the bottom and gentle slopes of the upper part of the Valley of the Volcanoes (phot. M. Wasilewski)

Fig. 28. Tuff deposits of the Alpabamba formation are often weathered into forms deceptively similar to those of Cappadocia. The height of the volcanic stocks, mushrooms and domes reaches up to 15–20 m (phot. A. Kukuła-Góral)

canic rock, generally composed of andesites: tuffs, lavas and ignimbrites. Some authors include these formations mentioned in the Tacaza Group, dividing it into a series of smaller units of the Neogene period (for example, Olchauski & Dávila 1994).

Formations of the already mentioned Alpabamba unit dominate in the area of the Valley of the Volcanoes. They create intermittent tuff coverings, in which obsidians appear here and there. The best-known and closest outcrops of the latter are the Alca deposits (probably the Chivay, as well). The Alpabamba tuffs, described both on this terrain and outside of it appear, as a rule, at altitudes higher than 4000 m a.s.l. Particularly large accumulations of them are found in the *puna* and in the valleys that cut into it between Pampa Atojoachana and the region of the Poracota mine on one side and the region of the Arcata municipality and lake of the same name on the other side. As seen in the field studies that have been carried out, the Alpabamba formation creates intermittent coverings and caps in the highest reaches of the valley slopes and, above all, in the *puna*, or precisely higher than 4000 m a.s.l.. Both of the formations described, as well as similar sediments of volcanic ash, are subject to intense water erosion and, in part, aeolian processes, creating their characteristic monadnock features (rock mushrooms, pillars, columns, cones and narrow, sharply-cut gullies, etc.), reminiscent of forms known from Anatolian Cappadocia (Fig. 28).

The somewhat younger Sencca formations (dacite and rhyolite lavas, tuffs and breccias) appear in the Valley of the Volcanoes in a similar geographical context (Paulo 2008). On the terrain described, however, there have not been found any of the Pliocene–Pleistocene andesite lavas or tuffs, conglomerates and sandstones of the Barroso Group that are found in neighboring areas, nor any sediments originating from their weathering (Olchauski & Dávila 1994).

To the west, north and also to the east and south of the Valley of the Volcanoes, large centers of the main Andean volcanism are found. The effect of this Pliocene–Pleistocene activity is seen in the high cones of Nevado Coropuna, Nevado Solimana, Nevado Firura, and somewhat farther to the southeast, beyond the incision of Colca Canyon – Nevado Ampato, Nevado Sabancaya and Hualca Hualca.

The most characteristic and distinctive element of the valley's morphology and geology is the young (Tertiary and Quaternary), alkaline volcanism (phenoandesite and basalt andesite lavas), which probably became dormant only 350–400 years ago. The large number of short (100–300 m in height) pyroclastic volcanic cones associated with it, appearing with surprising regularity (Fig. 5), were the reason for which the valley gained its modern name, Valle de los Volcanes. The picture is completed by the lava domes, difficult for the untrained eye to perceive, and also lava streams that cover the entire valley floor. The most recent of these, which plant life has not yet overgrown, resembles crests of

Fig. 29. The Alpabamba formation is made of delicately layered tuff coverings – Cotahuasi Valley (phot. M. Wasilewski)

Fig. 30. A cross-section of a small outcrop of the tuffs of Alpabamba in Cotahuasi Valley (phot. M. Wasilewski)

slag; at the same time, it is a serious obstacle to transportation (Gałaś & Paulo 2005). Older lavas, occurring mainly in the middle and upper reaches of the valley, have weathered and become overgrown with thorny grass, agaves and cactuses, and in places cultivated fields have even been established on them. There is no doubt that volcanic activity has influenced the river network of the valley, obstructing the flow of water in some places and instigating the formation of lakes (for example, Laguna Chachas). Both the *puna* and the upper part of the valley and its branches are also full of Quaternary glacial, fluvial, limnic and colluvial sediments.

Due to the substratum and surroundings, soils formed from lavas and volcanic ash dominate in the Valley of the Volcanoes, enriched here and there with material originating from the erosion of sedimentary rock of the surroundings. Just as in other parts of the high Andes, they have a small soil depth, not exceeding 20–25 cm (Lavallée 1985). These soils are relatively fertile (for example, creating on the andesites clay soils with magnesium and calcium), cultivation is hindered, however, by the low temperatures and above all the hard-to-access water. There is not the slightest doubt that both the course of the main river, as well as the morphology of the valley floor, have changed in historical times. This is proved by the traces of former riverbeds and

the localization of settlements and crop terraces on terrains that today are completely dry (for example, the Ayo region). These phenomena are connected with volcanic and tectonic activity in the Valley of the Volcanoes.

The most interesting among the many geological stratigraphic units that make up the Valley of the Volcanoes turned out to be, from the perspective of the studies conducted, the Alpabamba formation (Figs 29, 30). It forms acidic tuff sediments, in which here and there conditions for vitrification of silica and the appearance of obsidians have existed. Perhaps these points are connected with magma intrusions and domes (i.e. Cerro Pinta) which, originating underneath them or cutting across them, created the high temperatures that favor vitrification of tuff (see also Burger *et al.* 1998a, 1998b). The field studies were focused on the search for, mapping and description of precisely these places[8].

1.3. Outline of the sequence of climatic and cultural changes in Peru

An important factor forming the cultural picture of the first millennia of South America was the climate. The changes that occurred and certain permanent features of the

Andean biotopes are best traced on the basis of the palynological and paleobotanical records, and geological sediments. Around 14500 years B.P. (around 15500 cal B.C.), when the first traces of man appeared on the territory of today's Chile, Brazil, Venezuela and Peru (see below), nature began to enter the last episode of glaciation[9], although it was still warm and humid. The final disappearance of the Pleistocene glaciers, together with the decline of the Pleistocene occurred in the period 12600–11000 B.P. (around 13280–11050 cal B.C.). Compared to the present day, the climate then was a bit cooler, and the average annual air temperatures were lower, around 3–4.5°C. Only the beginning of the Holocene (around 11 050 cal B.C.) brought a clear warming and humidification, proceeding (with a transitional break 8250–7550 cal B.C.) to around 7000 cal B.C. and most likely continuing through the following millennia. It was certainly also in this period that the characteristic Andean cycle of seasons was also established (*austral summer-austral winter*). These changes resulted in the further disappearance of alpine glaciers, the rising of the ground water level and the appearance (also in the upper reaches of the Andes) of marshes and wetlands, along with the fauna that goes with it, including man (Aldenderfer 1998, Aldenderfer 2000, Wasilewski 2005).

From around 5850/5900 cal B.C. the amount of precipitation clearly decreased, but the temperatures remained rather high (Lynch 1980). Next – from around 4900/4650 cal B.C.[10] – a very dry episode in some areas (for example, in Ecuador), there began a period of rather abrupt climate change. This is connected with a phenomenon known today as El Niño-Southern Oscillation (ENSO)[11], which either appeared then for the first time, or else significantly intensified at that time. These phenomena directly influenced the state of flora and fauna in alpine areas as well, superimposing in part on the Holocene climate optimum to cause short-term periods of drought. More or less from 3900 cal B.C., the climate once again became somewhat cooler, but also more humid, stimulating the growth of the population of fauna, and thus also the hunter-gatherers in the Andes. It is thought that these conditions have been maintained until the present day (Aldenderfer 1998), although warmer and very cool episodes have been noted (the so-called *neo-glacial*, or Quechua phase, around 2500–500 cal B.C.; Szykulski 2005). All of these factors should be taken into account when considering the question of settlement of the *puna* areas, not only on the terrain of the Valley of the Volcanoes, for they influenced – and continue to influence – the biological productivity of the natural environment[12].

The cultural development of South America has been occurring since around 15 500 cal B.C.[13] (the so-called Paleoindian period). The earliest sites are believed to be: Monte Verde (Chile), Alice Boër (Brazil), Pedra Furada (Brazil), Lapa Vermelha IV (Brazil) and possibly Pikimachay (Peru) and Taima Taima (Venezuela). All of them, however, lie at low altitudes. The first traces of man's activity in the higher reaches of the Andes are dated only to around 13140 – 12100 cal B.C. (around 12500–12000 B.P.) and have been confirmed in the caves of Guitarrero (Peru, 2580 m a.s.l.), Lauricocha (Peru, 4050 m a.s.l.) and Telarmachay (Peru, 4450 m a.s.l.) (Lynch 1980, Rick 1980,

Lavallée 1985). Here, a small, very mobile group of hunter-gatherers took advantage of different food sources. Among these, it is worth mentioning: avifauna, small animals (guinea pigs, chinchillas and viscachas) as well as deer and vicugna, and also plants (perhaps tuberous roots and beans). Around five hundred years later, exploitation of these terrains had already become much more regular and with time began to be geared towards the use of camelids (first hunting, later increasing control and finally domestication). The groups acting in the *puna* zone also used central base sites, an example of which is actually the Lauricocha cave, as well as the Pachamachay[14] (Rick 1980). From the beginning, the connection between Andean hunters and obsidian is highlighted. Tools made from it, already in the beginning of the period, are of different sizes (including small and microlithic) with a series of morphological types distinguished among them (mainly concerning the projectile points). This entire period was characterized, however, by little changeability of culture, which intensified only with the domesti-cation of llamas (the turn of the sixth and fifth millennia B.C.) (Bruhns 1996).

In mountainous areas, there is a clearly visible transition from hunting and gathering to a gathering-livestock-agricultural economy, the standard example of which is the Guitarrero cave (Peru). At this site, in strata dated to around 10 400/9400 cal B.C. there have been found remains of what are considered to be domesticated beans. Some have cast doubt on this discovery, or mainly its ^{14}C dating, because it was based on the testing of charcoal present in the archaeological stratum, and not fragments of the plant itself (Pearsall 2003, Wasilewski 2005).

In the sixth millennium B.C. there most likely came about a complete dependency of man on one source of nourishment-livelihood: camelids (e.g. Lavallée 2000). Herds of these animals were at least kept under control at that time, even if they were not yet completely domesticated[15]. In more or less this same period, at somewhat lower altitudes, domestication of the dog (remains in the Uchcumachay cave) and guinea pig took place. There also appeared, on a large scale, a phenomenon which became one of the more characteristic elements of the economy of the Andes: "exploitation of verticality." This refers to the exchange of goods, typical of the Andes, between residents of different altitude zones, causing a bilateral flow mainly of agricultural products along the axis of valleys and the production specialization of particular groups of people (herders and hunters, farmers, farmer-"gardeners," fishermen) (see, for example, Burger *et al.* 1998b). At the time of the Early Horizon, this became one of the more important factors of cultural development[16].

As for the earliest traces of man in the vicinity of the Valley of the Volcanoes, the most interesting is the report of confirmation of Alca-1 obsidians at the maritime site of Quebrada Jaguay (Arequipa Province, Camaná District). This has been dated to the period of 11105 – 9850 B.P. (11180 – 9250 cal B.C.), which proves at least equally early visits to Cotahuasi Valley (Sandweiss *et al.* 1998, Burger *et al.* 2000, Jennings & Glascock 2002). From the vicinity of the obsidian outcrops located there, access to the nearby *puna* between Cotahuasi Valley and the Valley of the Volcanoes is relatively easy. There thus exists the possibility of such early penetration of this area. The oldest artifacts from Cotahuasi Valley itself, testifying to the more regular presence of man, originated however only in the mid-Paleoindian period (around 8250/5500 cal B.C.), from sites in the vicinity of the present-day city of Puica (Jennings & Glascock 2002). Later, obsidian of the Alca type already appeared in all sites of the region, all the way up to the Late Horizon.

We cannot apply all of this knowledge, however, directly to the Valley of the Volcanoes, as there is a lack of both archaeological evidence as well as precise dating. This is not, after all, a problem unique to the terrain of our studies. Even now, the statement that *"...Virtually nothing is known of the preceramic eras in the southern highlands, including the altiplano..."* (Bruhns 1996, p.72) is still accurate, and our interpretations are based on a wide extrapolation of very modest data.

From 2100 cal B.C. (the Preceramic/Initial period), developed societies appeared on the coast, building, among other things, centers of cult (Bruhns 1996). In the mountains during this time, there occurred a growth in the significance of raising llamas and alpacas. In the *puna* zone, there appeared numerous pastoral groups, who without a doubt enriched their diet with wild game and local plants (species of tuberous roots) and plants that came from exchange within the valley. Connected with this period are the latest discoveries of the remains of domesticated potatoes and corn at the Waynuna site (on the Cerro Aycano above Cotahuasi Valley), and thus in the immediate vicinity of the Valley of the Volcanoes, dated to around 2000/1700 cal B.C. (Perry *et al.* 2006). Some researchers, after all, suggest the view that it were pastoral-hunting groups that began to move and settle in the lower parts of valleys (Neira Avendaño 1998), changing into a settled, agricultural society.

In the Initial period (3750–2750 B.P. = around 2130–900 cal B.C.) there appeared one more important cultural phenomenon – ceramic. Closest to our terrains are the Initial traditions (styles) of Hachas (Acari Valley), Ayawala (Chuquibamba District, Condesuyos Province), Chanapata and Qaluyu from the area of Cusco and Chiripa from the Titicaca Basin (Bruhns 1996). All of these styles of ceramic production (with the exception of Hachas) have, perhaps, common roots in the Cusco-Titicaca zone (Szykulski 2005).

The majority of the most important processes that were occurring later in the so-called Central Andean cultural area, described with increasing precision in the literature on the subject, do not directly concern the region of the Valley of the Volcanoes. In the Early Horizon (2750–2050 B.P. = around 900–50 cal B.C.) the most important events took place in the north of what is now Peru (the appearance and development of the so-called Chavín Horizon) and the central part of the coast (Paracas and Nazca traditions). The Early Intermediate Period (2050–1400 B.P. = around 50 cal B.C. – 650 cal A.D.) is the time of the Moche culture's domination in the north and the development of the Wankarani, Chiripa and Pucara cultures in the basins of Lake Titicaca and Lake Poopó. However, only the establishment, blossoming and competition of the Wari (Huari) and Tiahuanaco empires (the so-called Middle Horizon: 1400–1050

B.P. = around 650–995 cal A.D.) left its mark in the archaeological record of the area of our study.

The Late Intermediate Period (1050–1476 A.D. = around 995–1476 cal A.D.), was characterized by balcanisation of culture (there appeared then, among other things, such units as Ica, Chimu and Chancay), preceding the great unification of Andean terrains within the Inca empire (the so-called Late Horizon, 1476–1532). The brief period of Inca rule and the first decades of the Conquistadors are relatively well-represented in the Valley of the Volcanoes.

1.4. Archaeology, history and ethnography of the Valley of the Volcanoes

To date, there have not been any systematic surface studies or organized inventory of archaeological sites conducted in the Valley of the Volcanoes. It is thus, from an archaeological perspective, almost an untouched territory. Sites from this area mentioned in the literature are known thanks to rather random reconnaissance activities (for example, E. Linares Málaga, M. Neira Avendaño[17]). A Polish-Peruvian expedition called *Proyecto Condesuyos*, led by A. Belan Franco and M. Ziółkowski[18], is only now being prepared to undertake an archaeological survey of the valley (Ziółkowski *et al.* 2000–2001, 2005, 2007). Now, in the literature on the subject, one can find only brief descriptions or mentioning of the following archaeological sites:

Antaymarca (Andahua District) – a site discovered in 1981, described as a ceremonial-burial ground (around 5 ha, Fig. 31). Presently situated on it are the remains of rectangular, stone buildings, perhaps also burials. Suggested dating: Late Intermediate Period (Linares Málaga 1991–1992).

Soporo-Maucallacta (Andahua District) – a site discovered in the 1980s, described as residential with an accompanying burial ground (around 3 ha). Remains of buildings in a rectangular layout have been documented there, as well as round (oval), subterranean and semi-subterranean burials and rectangular ones of the *chullpa*[19] type. Fragments of Incan ceramics have been found on the site. Suggested dating: Late Intermediate Period/Late Horizon (Linares Málaga 1991–1992). Another opinion on the topic of Soporo is expressed by Maximo Neira Avendaño, who, based on the presence of Hachas-type ceramic, and a new, Soporo-type (distinguished by himself, and considered to be early, due to the shape of the pots and their decoration with deep horizontal and slanted incisions, punctations and stamping of the "ring with a point" type) dates it to the Formative Period (more precisely – from around 1400 cal B.C. or even 1500 cal B.C.), by analogy to the Hachas site in the Acari District, Caraveli Province (Neira Avendaño 1998). Of course, it cannot be ruled out that both claims are true and the site was settled continuously – or, more likely, with breaks – throughout this entire period.

Paccareta or Pajareta (Andahua District) – a site discovered in the 1960s, is described as a site with petroglyphs. A hypothesis has been suggested about its connection with the Folsom complex, as there has been found there a triangular projectile point with a slightly concave base, described as the so-called *pseudofluted* or Lindenmeier type (Linares Málaga 1991–1992), however this attribute is rather doubtful.

Fig. 31. A view of the Antaymarca site from the northwest (phot. M. Wasilewski)

Fig. 32. A ruined tomb on the Ayapuraca site (Pumajollo), between Andahua and Chachas (phot. M. Wasilewski)

Fig. 33. Abandoned cultivated terraces on the Jello Jello site above the contemporary municipality of Ayo (phot. M. Wasilewski)

Besides those above, there are other sites mentioned only by name: Ayapuraca (=Pumajollo, Andahua District; Fig. 32), Ninamama, Capillayoc. In relation to these (particularly to the last two), there is a lack of any sort of more exact descriptions (Linares Málaga 1991–1992). In the lower part of the Valley of the Volcanoes in the Ayo District, there are three known localities with the remains of cultivated terraces, architecture and tombs (perhaps of the same age and connected with each other, the so-called Maucallacta, Jello Jello and Chaye Tollo ruins; Fig. 33). On the slopes at the border of Canión Colca and Valle de los Volcanes, there are visible remains of the first transportation routes, which can most likely be tied to the Late Horizon (Inca Period) or even older periods. They are not contemporarily used, as they have undergone shifting and movement in many places as a result of earthquakes and slope erosion. In the end, on the territory of some contemporary municipalities (for example, Andahua), different artifacts are found (for example, obsidian projectile points, ceramics such as Chuquibamba, zoomorphic figures).

It is also highly likely that the gold mine in the vicinity of Orcopampa, which was exploited by the Spanish and continues to be used today, was already known in Inca times or even earlier. Unfortunately, no traces have been saved of this possibly oldest mining activity: firstly due to the significant, anthropological transformation of the terrain in connection with historical and contemporary extraction activity, and secondly due to the nature of primitive mining, which was certainly based only on exploitation of placer de-

posits (colluvial and alluvial). Above the city of Orcopampa, a cemetery functions (so-called Ciminterio Sarpane, from the name of the village to which it belongs), in which the local population often unearths different obsidian tools and flakes[20] (Fig. 34). Located somewhat above this place, on the orographically left slope of the valley, are the remains of a round, stone structure considered by the locals to be a burial[21]. A few bone fragments lie about in the middle of it (for example, fragments of cranial vault), however there is a lack of any sort of grave goods, and the locals do not associate this site with the "*abuelo* cult" known from other territories[22].

Thus, in the Valley of the Volcanoes, there are known pre-Incan and Incan ruins, remains of cultivated terraces, roads and cemeteries. Unfortunately, some of them are undergoing progressive destruction as a result of earthquakes and volcanic activity, but also due to the activities of the local population. Dating of the sites is based on simplified references to other parts of Peru, however there is a lack of any kind of systematic study and dating in the Valley itself.

The exploratory work conducted by the author was aimed, above all, at locating and describing obsidian deposits. Thus, from an archaeological perspective, it is also highly random and incomplete, as it is limited by necessity to the recording of sites and individual findings encountered during the above-mentioned survey. However, this does not change the fact that this has been, so far, the only study of this type in the upper parts of the Valley of the Volcanoes. It has even greater value, considering the fact that traces of

Fig. 34. Obsidian and chalcedony stone tools found in the Valley of the Volcanoes and surrounding area, accumulated at the school in Soporo (phot. M. Wasilewski)

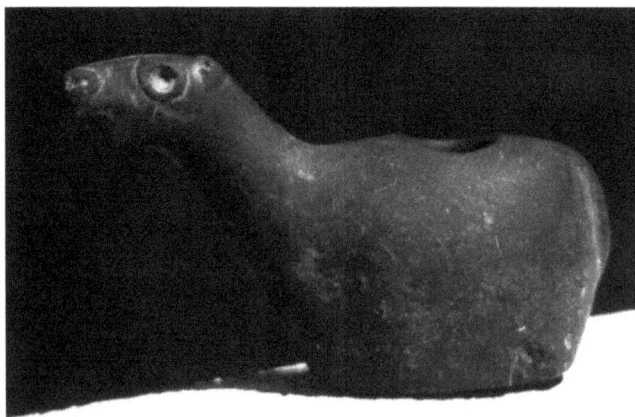

Fig. 35. A figure representing a llama, originating in the Late Period, kept in the mayoralty of Andahua (phot. M. Wasilewski)

human activity in the *puna* region have, in large part, the character of surface sites. As a result of this, stone tools (mainly projectile points) and larger fragments of them are gathered by the local population and – at best – kept in local "museums" (schools, mayoralties, etc.; Fig. 34), and as a rule are kept in homes or sold to visitors. Other artifacts such as ceramics, sculptures, fabrics (Figs 32, 35) encounter a similar fate. Together with the growth of tourism, this procedure is gaining in strength and the possibility of locating and describing local sites is irrevocably lost[23].

As already mentioned, the deficiency of studies and the destructive processes in the region discussed do not allow the full reconstruction of its history. It will thus be presented only as a general outline on the basis of analogy to neighboring territories, and above all to the prehistory of southern Peru. One must remember, however, that reconnaissance in other areas, as well, has a "spotty" nature, and there exist large regions completely deprived of even a preliminary archaeological examination (Rick 1996, Aldenderfer 1998, Szykulski 2005).

How the first settlers arrived on the territory of the Valle de los Volcanes, as well as the time of this event are unknown. It might have been a route leading in from the coast, although one should rather take into account migration from neighboring high-mountain terrains that had been settled earlier, mainly from Cotahuasi Valley (Burger *et al.* 1998b, Jennings & Glascock 2002). Early migrations from Colca Valley are rather doubtful (Burger *et al.* 2000). In the first of the valleys mentioned, there are known, rich deposits of obsidian in the vicinity of the Alca municipality (so-called *Alca obsidian*). It is known that this raw material had been used since the Preceramic Period over a very extensive area (Burger *et al.* 2000).

Passing over the supposition mentioned, but so far unconfirmed, as to the presence of the first hunters visiting the Alca deposits in the vicinity of and within the Valle de los Volcanes itself already around 12 100 cal B.C.[24], it is suspected that the first humans appeared on the territory of interest only in the Late Preceramic Period[25] (around 6150–3640 B.P. = around 5050–2015 cal B.C.; Soporo site) (Neira Avendaño 1998) or even in the Initial Period (3750–2750 B.P. = around 2130–900 cal B.C.) (Bruhns 1996). One of the sites considered to be the earliest, located on the edge of the Valley of the Volcanoes and confirming this hypothesis, is Arcata (Condesuyos Province, Cayarani District), whose age was estimated by its discoverer (G. Schroeder) to be approximately 6000–4000 B.C.[26] (around 7050–4900 cal B.C.). Other researchers are inclined, however, to date this site to a more recent period than 4900 cal B.C. (Schobinger 1988), unfortunately, there is a lack of radiocarbon dating in this case. Among other things that have been described there are the very characteristic *perforadores de muleta* as well as a small, triangular projectile point (for an arrow?) (Schobinger 1988), which appear also on sites located by the author (see chapters II.2 and II.4; for example, Figs 41, 43) and are usually associated with the later periods.

The next traces of man in the Valley of the Volcanoes are connected only with the Initial Period. Namely, there have been found in the valley fragments – considered to be rather early – of Hachas-type ceramic (Soporo-Maucallacta; Neira Avendaño 1990, 1998), which are perhaps the traces of their creators' expansion (Szykulski 2005). On this same site, there have also been extracted pieces of ceramic, described by Neira Avendaño as the Soporo type, to which an equally early or only slightly younger chronology is attributed (Neira Avendaño 1990, 1998).

Unfortunately, little is known on the topic of the history of the Valley of the Volcanoes in the period of the Early Horizon (2750–2050 B.P. = around 900–50 cal B.C.) and in the Early Intermediate Period (2050–1400 B.P. = around 50 cal B.C. – 650 cal A.D.). Most likely, some of the archaeological traces have been subject to obliteration as a result of volcanic activity (just as, certainly, the remains of other periods). One can only suspect that the development of large cultural-trade centers, both on the coast (Chavín de Huántar, Paracas, and then Recuay, Moche, Nazca and others), as well as mainly in the mountains (in the vicinity of Lake Titicaca Wankarani, Chiripa and then Pucara, Tiahuanaco), was not without influence on the area of our study (surely settled by agricultural and pastoral societies), especially if the local deposits of gold were already known at that time. During this whole time, the use of obsidian deposits was also intensifying both in Alca and in Chivay, which certainly generated human activity also in our area of interest[27] (Burger *et al.* 2000).

When in the so-called Middle Horizon (1400–1050 B.P. = around 650–995 cal A.D.) the Tiahuanaco and Wari (Huari) empires arose in the Andes, the Valley of the Volcanoes found itself in the area of contact and interaction of both units mentioned (Neira Avendaño 1990, Neira Avendaño 1998). This territory is counted today among the cultural provinces of the Central and South-central Andes (Andes Centrales, Andes Centro-Sur), as likewise the neighboring Colca Valley. The Cotahuasi area was under the tight control of Wari, which in conjunction with the ease of access to the Valle de los Volcanes, might have been the cause of its occupation precisely by this empire (Burger *et al.* 2000). There likely appeared at that time in the Valley more permanent transportation-trade routes, extensive cultivated terraces (mainly for corn and coca), an irrigation network and the settlements known today as the sites Antaymarca, Soporo and Jello Jello (?). After the fall of the Wari, there occurred a thinning out of the network of settlements and movement of people (Bruhns 1996).

Once more, the history of the Valley is not clear in the Late Intermediate Period (1050 B.P.–1476 A.D. = around 995–1476 cal A.D.), when in other parts of Peru the Chimu, Chancay and Inca cultures were arising. During this whole time, the Valley of the Volcanoes was found in the area of contact among different cultural units of Chuquibamba (of which the native area was the nearby contemporary province of Condesuyos) and Churajón (situated mainly in the Tambo River basin, and also in the valley of the Chili River). It was most likely penetrated by, above all, the population of the Chuquibamba culture, a testament to which can be seen in the fragments of Chuquibamba ceramic (so-called *polícromo*) found, for example, in Antaymarca or Andahua[28]. These are mainly bowls (*cuencos*), deep plates, cups, tall pots (*ollas altas*), jugs (*cantaros*), all with decora-

tions made in red and reddish-brown color, sometimes with a black or white line, in the shape of rhombuses, circles or triangles. Representations of the sun, birds, llamas and sometimes humans are also known. On the edges of pots there are painted bands decorated with motifs of the heads of foxes and/or ducks (Neira Avendaño 1990, Neira Avendaño 1998, Szykulski 2005). It is also known that over this entire time, obsidian was an important raw material for producing weapons and hunting implements, which generated an interest in its deposits in the vicinity of Alca (Burger & Asaro 1997, Jennings & Glascock 2002).

Situated above the Valle de los Volcanes, the Coropuna Volcano (Fig. 94), which had been worshipped even earlier (Chuquibamba(?), Collaguas people), maintained, or even increased in the period of Inca domination (Late Horizon, 1476–1532 A.D.) the status of the important place of cult (Ziółkowski *et al.* 2000–2001, 2005, 2007; Szykulski 2005). This special function undoubtedly influenced the degree of penetration of the surrounding territories, including the Valley of the Volcanoes. The gold deposits found in the upper parts of the valley were an additional magnet. All of these circumstances mean that in the archaeological record of the Valley of the Volcanoes, there remain clear traces (Fig. 35), despite the decline of interest in obsidian as a raw material. Some sites should be associated with this period, such as at least the terrain of the present city of Andahua, and perhaps also the Jello Jello site. The transportation-trade routes that were already mentioned, as well as other elements of infrastructure, were undoubtedly built up, reconstructed or developed.

Still in the first centuries of Spanish domination, the Valley of the Volcanoes was visited due to the gold mines taken over from the Incas. However, after the gold deposits accessible at that time were exhausted, it fell into oblivion. The whole time, only very rare settlement by farmers and – in the upper parts – herders appeared in it. The Valley was once again "discovered" by two travelers and researchers connected with the National Geographic Society: Robert Shippee and George R. Johnson. They happened upon this region in the 1930s during one of their reconnaissance and photography flights, landing both in the Valle de los Volcanes, as well as in the neighboring Cotahuasi Valley (Shippee & Johnson 1934). Since the 1980s, intensive geological-exploratory work and documentation in connection with gold mining have been conducted in the upper parts of the Valley of the Volcanoes. Other works besides these have arisen in the course of preparing a Masters thesis (Portocarrero 1960), preliminary regional studies (Hoempler 1962) and small tourist folders (from the years 2004/ 2005).

Not all of the Valley of the Volcanoes offers terrains suitable for cultivation. They are concentrated today mainly around existing municipalities. The lowest-situated of these are the cultivated fields of Ayo, and then the next are found only around the municipalities of Sucna, Chachas, Soporo, Andahua (together with the Pampa Colao Colo and Pampa Charca) in the central part of the valley (Figs 6, 9). The next terrains with agricultural significance extend from Chapacoco to Chilcaimarca and Orcopampa (Fig. 7), and the small fields above Orcopampa in the direction of the Umachulco

Fig. 36. The llamas and alpacas that are grazed in the puna zone are shy animals and to this day are moderately watched over by man (phot. M. Wasilewski)

Valley. On the eastern side of the valley, in its upper reaches, cultivation is encountered only in the region of the Pampa Panahua icefalls. Most level areas above Andahua (as a rule, called *la pampa*) and the *puna* terrains (for example, Pampa Jararanca, Pampa de Antapuna, Pampa Atojoachana) are used for grazing llamas and alpacas (Fig. 36).

In particular parts of the valley, various species of plants are cultivated, depending on climatic conditions. In the *quechua* (where crops can be harvested more than once a year), corn, wheat, pumpkins, caigua (*Cyclanthera pedata*), sweet granadilla (*Passiflora ligularis*), beans, peppers and *rocoto* (*Capsicum* sp. and *Capsicum pubescens*), tomatoes, papayas, avocados and many other plants adapted to mild temperature regimes are cultivated today (and formerly, for example, the coca plant – *Erythroxylon coca*). In a higher zone – the *suni* – cultivation is more difficult, and in the contemporary species structure, the dominant position is occupied by: *saúco peruano*, or rayan (*Sambucus peruviana*, a tree with edible fruits), cantuta (*Cantua buxifolia*, the so-called flower of the Incas), Quinoa (also called Incan rice, *Chenopodium quinoa*), Andean lupin (*Lupinus mutabilis*), and four important plants that provide edible tubers: potatoes (*Solanum tuberosum*), oca (*Oxalis tuberosa*), ulluco (*Ullucus tuberosus*) and mashua (*Tropeolum tuberosum*, also called *isañu*). In the *puna,* only some species of potatoes and quinoa are cultivated, moreover the stipa (ichu), fruits of the Indian fig opuntia (*Opuntia ficus-indica*) and maca (*Lepidium meyenii*) which grow in the wild are also used (Bruhns 1996, Brack 2003). In all zones the *queñoa* tree (*Polylepis rugulosa*) can be encountered. Another very widespread species of tree, introduced by the Spanish after extermination of the local mountain cypress (*Austrocedrus chilensis*), is the less noble eucalyptus (*Eucalyptus* sp.). Also foreign are grains such as the common oat (*Avena sativa*) and barley (*Hordeum vulgare*) as well as alfalfa (*Medicago sativa*).

The wood of the *queñoa*, quite hard and durable, has been used for building houses, making tools and for fuel. The *ichu* grass is used even today as a roof covering. The apiales *la yareta* (Fig. 19) finds application in treating respi-

Fig. 37. Domesticated animals in the area of the Andes: a) llama (*Lama glama*); b) alpaca (*Lama pacos*); c) guinea pig (*Cavia tschudii*) (phot. M. Wasilewski)

ratory disorders (in a pulverized form) and diabetes, and also in a dried form as an excellent fuel (today, however, this plant is formally found under special protection). Some of the plants have medical applications confirmed in original texts and in ethnography. These are, for example, the joint fir (*Ephedra americana*), bidens (*Bidens andicola*), *Mutisia acuminata*, some species of ragworts (*Senecio* sp.), *Perezia coerulesceus* (*sutuma* or *escorzonera*), cantuta (*Cantua buxifolia*), huamanpinta (*Chuquiraga spinosa*) and others (Żurowska 2001, Brack 2003).

Domesticated animals of the Valley of the Volcanoes are, just as in other parts of Peru, the llama (*Lama glama*),

Fig. 38. Fertility rituals are often ordered by every family separately from a professional "officiator"; Chilcaymarca municipality (phot. M. Wasilewski)

alpaca (*Lama pacos*) and guinea pig (*Cavia tschudii*) (Fig. 37 a-c). In every part of the valley (except for the highest-positioned settlements), guinea pigs, chickens and recently also trout are raised. Sheep, horses and cattle appeared only from the time that the Spanish arrived. The extent of cattle-raising reaches to an altitude of around 3500 m above sea level. Above that, llamas and alpacas are kept, and since colonial times also sheep. The peregrine falcon (*Falco peregrinus*) hunts on cultivated terrains, as well as several other species of predatory birds.

Exchange between cultivation zones, universally present even today, was also the main way of satisfying the population's nutritional needs in the past. Trade exchange encompassed plants, as well as animal products (mainly wool, fabrics and meat) and ceramics.

Only in the last two decades of the XX century A.D. did modernity enter the Valley of the Volcanoes: vehicular transport, electricity, telephone and internet, mass-produced food, non-traditional building materials (sheet metal, fired brick, glass, etc.). However, despite the rapid Westernization of culture, the local societies have maintained elements of pre-Christian traditions to the present day. This is observed both among the local population, as well as the migrant population (miners). Each of the newly-built houses is consecrated by a priest, but besides that, a traditional building sacrifice is made from a llama or its blood for *Pachamama* (Mother Earth[29]). Homes that have been destroyed by lightening are left alone as a place occupied by the god of lightening, called Illapa by the Incas (Bolin 2002; there are

also extensive descriptions of other rituals of this type). Here and there, cults of mummies are also encountered, called by the locals *abuelo* (grandfather), and considered to be ancestor-guardians (Rogozińska 2008). An interesting tradition is the offering of nature's bounty (corn, llama fat, coca, alcohol) to the Mother Earth and *Mamacocha* (the goddess of surface waters and fertility), in the course of a nighttime fertility ritual at which *chicha* freely flows (Bolin 2002; Fig. 38). In the Valley, feast days (*fiestas*) typical for Peru are regularly held in connection with various religious and secular occasions (for example, the feast day of the settlement). Sometimes they are associated with folk competitions, like the competition of fabrics and embroidery that takes place in Chachas, as the local population produces a large part of ceramics and fabrics on its own the whole time (Fig. 39).

Just as in most territories of Peru, the cultivation of coca is forbidden today also in the Valley of the Volcanoes. However, the custom of chewing leaves of this plant is widespread, especially among older people and shepherds. This is not surprising when we realize that in these difficult environmental conditions, coca prevents the effects of altitude sickness, and also dulls the sense of hunger and maintains a state of stimulation.

The difficulty mentioned in access to medicine (see chapter I.1) is, in turn, one of the reasons for the unusual popularity of traditional medicine. It has both a magical element, as well as pharmaceutical. The whole palette of means derived from plants, animals and minerals, with

Fig. 39. Spinning wool is traditionally a women's task, however weaving and crocheting remain in some regions a male domain; Colca Valley, Chivay (phot. M. Wasilewski)

faith, conviction and most often good results, is used both by the highland herders, the valley farmers and also mine workers of all levels. Their effectiveness and the foundations for their use are also proved by contemporary scientific studies (Wasilewski 2008, Wasilewski 2009).

2. RESEARCH CARRIED OUT IN THE VALLEY OF THE VOLCANOES

2.1. Subject, purpose and methods of research. Area of research

The poor reconnaissance of the region of the Valley of the Volcanoes offers a large possibility for exploration. Both the residents and the provincial authorities have accepted with interest the Polish initiative of creating a National Park in the Valley of the Volcanoes and Colca Canyon, the deepest in the world. The research that was conducted is intended for preparing the scientific documentation that is indispensible for proclaiming the above-mentioned National Park. In this territory with sparse vegetation, rock formations are perfectly revealed and it is precisely this geological heritage that deserves protection. The position of the Valley of the Volcanoes (Fig. 1) between two very important centers of obsidian exploitation in Alca (Cotahuasi Valley) and Chivay (Colca Valley) also makes it an attractive terrain for geo-archaeological and archaeologi-

cal exploration (Burger *et al.* 1998a, Burger *et al.* 1998b, Burger *et al.* 2000, Jennings & Glascock 2002, Glascock *et al.* 2007). This research is all the more promising given that this area is also, in these respects, practically unstudied and, moreover, it hosts a series of plateaux of the *puna* zone and extensive intermountain valleys that are considered to be one of the basic biotopes of hunter-gatherer groups and, later, herders. All of these factors influenced the decision to undertake field surveys precisely in the Valley of the Volcanoes[30].

The raw material used by man in the past and analyzed by the author – obsidian – is a volcanic glass composed in large part of silica (SiO_2), aluminum oxide (Al_2O_3). Na_2O, K_2O, Fe_3O_4, water (H_2O) and other admixtures make up around 1%. This rock originates as a result of sudden cooling of acidic lavas of high viscosity, and also the heating up, re-melting and also the immediate cooling of acidic volcanic ash – tuffs. This is also a frequent ingredient of hot ash streams – lahars. Obsidian is mainly black or gray, and from transparent to translucent. There also occur specimens that are reddish or greenish, bi- or tri-colored, striped or spotted, opaque, and with fluidal textures. Different colors and textures are determined by admixtures of chromophores (for example, chrome, iron), the presence of inclusions and fractures, and the physical-chemical conditions that predominate in the course of their formation. The genesis factors mentioned determine the presence and mutual proportions of different ingredients, including especially accessory and trace elements (Ba, Cs, Rb, Sr, Hf, Sb, Th, etc.). It is precisely these features which are highly characteristic for particular deposits and allow them to be distinguished from each other (Glascock *et al.* 2007). It is assumed that this composition remains unchanged for the entire time of the obsidian's existence[31], which enables the detailed characterization of particular outcrops, and also of archaeological artifacts.

Obsidian deposits are not uncommon in the Andes. Among the best-known are Alca, Chivay, Quispisisa, and also Puzolana, Jampatilla, the Potreropampa region and Aconcahua (Burger & Asaro 1977, Burger *et al.* 1998a, Burger *et al.* 1998b, Burger & Glascock 2000a and 2000b, Jennings & Glascock 2002, Glascock *et al.* 2007). Obsidian, like glass, has excellent technological properties that predestine it for making tools (for example, a hardness of around 5.5 on the Mohs scale). Its drawback is, unfortunately, is that it is very brittle. Today, it is considered an ornamental stone and is readily used in jewelry-making, although obsidian blades are sometimes used in heart and blood vessel surgery.

In the course of the research undertaken in 2004 and continued in 2005, practically the entire hollow of the Valley was studied, as well as the plateaux surrounding it and side valleys. The first season (June – August 2004) was devoted mainly to reconnaissance of the terrain, confrontation of geological maps with the natural realty and preparation of work for the next year. In 2004, several new archaeological surface sites were also located, those already mentioned in the literature (see I.3) were visited, and the main obsidian-bearing formations (the so-called *formación* Alpabamba) were surveyed. For the purpose of comparison, the

Alca and Chivay deposits were also visited. All of this undertaking was realized as part of a larger project: Scientific Expedition AGH Peru – Valley of the Volcanoes 2004 (director A. Paulo[32]). The next stage (June – August 2005), had the aim of surveying deposits/outcrops of obsidian, the extent of which, thanks to earlier-conducted studies and analyses, has been limited to the upper part of the Valley (the vicinity of Orcopampa), side valleys, and above all plateaux in the *puna* zone. Besides geological maps, satellite photos and interviews with local geologists (from the gold mine Buenaventura-Orcopampa[33]), field reconnaissance and inteviewes carried out together with the local people was unusually useful.

The purpose of both research seasons was to answer the question as to whether obsidian deposits exist in the Valley of the Volcanoes, how many there are, in which part of the Valley and in which geological formations they are located. Information was also gathered on the topic of their character (primary, secondary), abundance, quality, possibilities and signs of their use, and the difference from and similarity to the Alca and Chivay deposits. Additionally, an explanation was sought for the genesis of this type of deposit. Archaeological surface sites were documented along the way, when the occasion presented itself, which explains (along with time limitations and the fact that most of the work, including the field studies, was conducted by the author alone) the great incompleteness of the registration of this record. Despite these inconveniences, an attempt was made to examine the connections between the artifacts found (sites) and the Alca, Chivay and local deposits. This aspect of the work (survey) undoubtedly requires continuation in accordance with the rules of archaeological survey, however this remains in the jurisdiction of the Polish-Peruvian mission, *Proyecto Condesuyos* acting in this territory.

In the course of both seasons, the search was carried out in this difficult-to-access area mostly on foot, seldom taking advantage of the transport offered by the Buenaventura concern[34]. All points were located with the assistance of a GPS 300 Magellan device and were introduced onto a map, giving them unique identification symbols. The materials were gathered by taking several to several tens of samples of material (natural fragments, as well as flakes and tools or their fragments) into labelled bags.

In studying the gathered materials, 75 fragments were set apart for NAA and XRF analysis, and identified by the numbers WAS001–WAS075[35] (according to the requirements of the laboratory carrying out the tests). Next, each sample was divided into the categories mentioned above (natural fragments, flakes and tools or their fragments). All of the tools and their fragments have been sketched.

The method of NAA (Neutron Activation Analysis) used to analyze the samples is one of the most qualitatively and quantitatively precise instrumental analyses standardly applied in different studies of materials science. With the help of this method, it is possible to determine the basic elemental composition of the analyzed sample, but above all, to study the type and quantity of trace elements. From among the many possibilities of its application, the one of greatest interest from the perspective of this study is the fingerprint analysis which, today, is routinely done on obsid-

ian. It enables the attribution of a concrete sample (natural fragment or an artifact) to a concrete source of origin (as long as it is found, of course, in the database of the laboratory which conducts the analysis) and the determination of its relationship to other finds, precisely on the basis of the chemical elements it is composed of. This method, combined with field studies, allows also for the detailed definition of new sources of obsidian.

Neutron activation analysis depends on the phenomenon of the emission of β particles and γ radiation by the sample when it is bombarded with free neutrons. The source of neutrons is a nuclear reactor. As a result of the collision of emitted particles with the nuclei of atoms contained in the sample, radioactive isotopes arise, with a short half-life of decay. As a result of the latter, the above-mentioned emission of β particles and γ radiation occurs. The recording of both of these, but mainly the latter, is the basis for determining the elemental composition of the studied sample. This is because each of the elements has a strictly characteristic (unique) energy of gamma radiation, and the number of its waves per unit time (intensity), in turn gives the premise for determining the content (quantity) of an element in the sample.

The tests were carried out in the Research Reactor Center University of Missouri-Columbia USA by Michael D. Glascock. The seventy-five samples selected by the author for these tests were subjected to two-stage XRF – NAA analysis. The first of these (X-Ray Fluorescence), first used in relation to obsidian in the beginning of the 1970s by Richard Burger, is a classic X-ray analysis. The sample, illuminated with X-rays, emits a spectrum of waves with intensity depending on its elemental composition. This preliminary test sometimes allows one, given the present degree of familiarity with obsidian deposits, to determine the sample's place of origin. For this analysis, an Elva-X spectrometer with a rhodium anode was used. The time of measurement was 400 seconds, and the results were processed with the help of the program Elva-X Analysis Package. The set of elements whose content was determined is seen in the tables presented below.

In the case of ambiguity or the impossibility of a final evaluation for the studied object, resulting from the limitations of the XRF method, the NAA was additionally used. To conduct this test, the sample is first washed with water before grinding in an agate mortar. 100 or 200 mg is measured out and mixed with cellulose glue in a proportion of 2:1. Next, tablets are formed (1×0.12 cm), covered with a thin layer of polyamide (0.0025 cm) and placed in a special tray (24 tablets at a time). The samples, thus prepared, are twice bombarded with streams of neutrons. The first time, this lasts 5 seconds ($8E13$ n/cm^{-2}/s^{-1}), after which proceeds cooling (25 minutes) and counting or measurement (12 minutes). With the help of a germanium detector, the gamma radiation that results from the presence of Al, Cl, Dy, K, Mn and Na is recorded. In the second stage of the test, the sample is subjected to radiation by a stream of neutrons with a density of $5E13$ n/cm^{-2}/s^{-1} for fifty hours. Next, the tablets are cooled for eight days, the radiation emitted by them is recorded in a 30-minute session and they are cooled again, this time for 30 days. The final counting lasts 2.5 hours for each sample. Such a procedure allows mistakes to be avoided and at the same time makes it possible to gain the most information on the composition of each sample (Burger & Asaro 1977, Glascock 2006). The NAA test is done on a MURR apparatus (Missouri University Research Reactor), calibrated on obsidians of known origin (Alca, Chivay, Quispisisa and others) from the university collection.

2.2. Results of field studies

During the two years of field work, 45 places in which obsidian appears were surveyed. These include outcrops, as well as archaeological sites and loose findings. Below, all of these points are ordered according to the sequence in which they were located in the field. The description includes the symbol given during field work, and then a precise characterization encompassing geographical coordinates, administrative jurisdiction and its position in the territory. The number and type of samples gathered is also given, dividing them into tools, flakes and geofacts (natural fragments). Sketches of the tools are also put in appropriate places. No statistical conclusions should be drawn on the basis of information concerning the number of samples as, for practical reasons, not all fragments of obsidian found in a concrete point were collected. Such action would have, above all, given rise to logistical problems: with regards to time (in some places, for example O.11, the number of obsidian fragments was very large), and transportation (the total weight of samples and the necessity of transporting them independently). Tools, in this case, were an exception – all of them were collected to the extent possible, by way of choosing the "lesser evil." The sites described are indeed difficult to access for the most part, however the material lying on the surface is often collected by the locals, which irrevocably disturbs their context and usually makes it impossible to correctly localize them again and to date them.

List of archaeological sites and loose findings described in the Valle de los Volcanes (see Map)

Label: 1
Date: 15.07.2004
Geographical coordinates: 15°28'10'' S / 72°20'54'' W / 3700 m a.s.l.
Administrative location: Arequipa Departament, Castilla Province, Andagua District **Geomorphology:** middle of valley bottom, path on the lava stream
Field-collected samples:
 – flakes: 1
Raw material: obsidian
Characteristics: neighbourhood of Paccareta (Pajareta) ruins; loose finding, no context, no outcrop
NAA (Neutron Activation Analysis): no

Label: 6-7
Date: 14.07.2004
Geographical coordinates: 15°30'54'' S / 72°20'22'' W / 3450 m a.s.l.
Administrative location: Arequipa Departament, Castilla Province, Andagua District, Antaymarca Site
Geomorphology: plane lava stream (promontory), covered with

weathered rock, above the river valley
Field-collected samples:
 – flakes: 2
Raw material: andesitic lava of Andagua Formation; chalcedony
Characteristics: local lava from ceremonial-cemetery site of Intermedio Tardio (?) age, and chalcedony flake
NAA: no

Label: 8
Date: 11.07.2004
Geographical coordinates: 15°40'58'' S / 72°16'19'' W / 1945–2000 m a.s.l.
Administrative location: Arequipa Departament, Castilla Province, Ayo District, Jello Jello Site
Geomorphology: lava stream slope, covered with weathered rock and terraced valley slopes
Field-collected samples:
 – flakes: 1
 – rock fragments: 1
Raw material: local andesitic lava of Andagua Formation
Characteristics: local raw materials from archaeological site
NAA: no

Label: CO
Date: 17.07.2004
Geographical coordinates: 15°29'05'' S / 72°20'03'' W / 3500 m a.s.l.
Administrative location: Arequipa Departament, Castilla Province, Andagua District
Geomorphology: western slope of valley-canyon, at the rock wall bottom
Field-collected samples:
 – flakes: 1
Raw material: chalcedony
Characteristics: neighbourhood of the Andagua River hanging bridge; loos finding, no context, no outcrop
NAA: no

Label: N-S and G/D
Date: 17.07.2004
Geographical coordinates: 15°28'54'' S – 15°29'05'' S / 72°20'11'' W – 72°20'03'' W / 3450–3400 m a.s.l.
Administrative location: Arequipa Departament, Castilla Province, Andagua District
Geomorphology: steep, western slope of valley-canyon
Field-collected samples:
 – tools: 1 chalcedony (retouched flake)
 – flakes and chips: 24
 – rock fragments: 11
Raw material: obsidian; chalcedony
Characteristics: neighbourhood of the Andagua River hanging bridge; loos findings, no context, in colluvia; no outcrop (covered with colluvia or very small)
NAA: yes (obsidian)

Label: O.1–O.4
Date: 19.07.2004
Geographical coordinates: 15°15'28'' S – 15°14'42'' S / 72°27'36'' W – 72°27'35'' W / 4540 m a.s.l.
Administrative location: Arequipa Departament, Castilla Province, Orcopampa District
Geomorphology: fluvio-glacial sediments on the plateau in *puna* zone, promontory and slope of the hill above marshy terrain
Field-collected samples:
 – tools: 2 (projectile point and bottom fragment of projectil point; Fig. 40)

– flakes: 3
– rock fragments: 1
Raw material: obsidian
Characteristics: SE part of Pampa Llulinsha; loos finding, archaeological site withplethora of flakes (mainly obsidian), approx. 400 m², no outcrop
NAA: yes

Label: O.5 and O.6
Date: 19.07.2004
Geographical coordinates: 15°18'41'' S / 72°27'04'' W / 4400 m a.s.l.
Administrative location: Arequipa Departament, Castilla Province, Orcopampa District, near Pabellon Mauras Vulcano
Geomorphology: alluvial sediments, sit in the river meander, plateau in the *puna* zone
Field-collected samples:
– tools: 1 (retouched flake)
– flakes: 1
– rock fragments: 1
Raw material: andesitic/basaltic lava, chalcedony
Characteristics: loose finding, no context, no outcrop
NAA: no

Label: O.8 and O.9
Date: 20.07.2004
Geographical coordinates: 15°12'31'' S / 72°19'27'' W / 4050–4150 m a.s.l.
Administrative location: Arequipa Departament, Castilla Province, Orcopampa District, Quisqaquisquayco (Huancarama)
Geomorphology: valley slope
Field-collected samples:
– flakes: 6
– rock fragments: 12
Raw material: chalcedony: white, gray, honey yellow, green, brown, black, red, colorless
Characteristics: silificated chalcedony vain in ignimbrite, slope gravels, no context, possible knapping site on the outcrop
NAA: no

Label: O.10
Date: 20.07.2004
Geographical coordinates: 15°12'31'' S / 72°19'27'' W / 4000 m a.s.l.
Administrative location: Arequipa Departament, Castilla Province, Orcopampa District
Geomorphology: valley slope
Field-collected samples:
– flakes: 1
Raw material: obsidian
Characteristics: below O.8 and O.9; loose finding, no context, no obsidian outcrop
NAA: no

Label: O.11
Date: 20.07.2004
Geographical coordinates: 15°05'45'' S / 72°20'16'' W / 4380 m a.s.l.
Administrative location: Arequipa Departament, Condesuyos Province, Cayarani District, between pueblo Quento and Calachane
Geomorphology: promontory between Chalhua Puqaio and Cochasique rivers, excellent view on the wide and watered inter-mountain dell
Field-collected samples:
– tools: 34 obsidian (15 projectil points and fragments, knife,

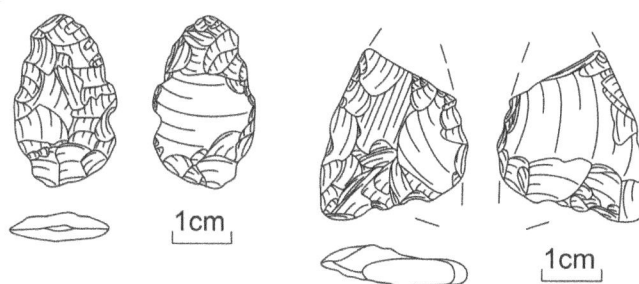

Fig. 40. Tools from O.1–O.4

3 end-scrapers, side-scraper, *pieces esquilles*, denticulated tool on *pieces esquilles*, burin (?) and 11 retouched flakes with *biface* (4) and *uniface* (7) retouche; Fig. 41) and 5 chalcedony (projectile point fragment, 3 end-scrapers, backed knife; Fig. 42)
– flakes and chips: obsidian 195, chalcedony 12
– rock fragments: obsidian 49, chalcedony 12
Raw material: obsidian black and red; chalcedony: white, honey yellow, black and red
Characteristics: large archaeological site, approx. 650 m²; no outcrop
NAA: yes (for obsidian)

Label: O.12
Date: 21.07.2004
Geographical coordinates: 15°21'15'' S – 15°21'36'' S / 72°16'28'' W – 72°17'38'' W / 4200–4300 m a.s.l.
Administrative location: Arequipa Departament, Castilla Province, Orcopampa District, neighbourhood of Panahua village
Geomorphology: promontory above plateau in *puna* zone
Field-collected samples: – tools: 13 obsidian (projectil point and fragment, 8 end-scrapers and fragments, side-scraper, *pieces esquilles* and retouched flake; Fig. 43) and 2 chalcedony (projectil point and fragment; Fig.44)
– flakes: obsidian 35, chalcedony 12
– rock fragments: obsidian 23, chalcedony 14
Raw material: obsidian black and red; chalcedony: white, brown, black, greenish, and red; andesitic lava of Andagua Formation
Characteristics: archaeological site, approx. 250 m², no outcrop
NAA: yes (for obsidian)

Label: D.01
Date: 24.07.2004
Geographical coordinates: 15°25'06'' S / 72°44'19'' W / 4290 m a.s.l.
Administrative location: Arequipa Departament, Condesuyos Province, Chuquibamba District, *pueblito* Arma
Geomorphology: plateau between Nevado Firura, Nevado Coropuna and Nevado Solimana, slopes and small promontory about 15 m above marshy terrain and stream bed
Field-collected samples:
– tools: 3 (projectile point fragment, *perforador de muleta*, retouched flake; Fig. 45)
– flakes: 11
– rock fragments: 10
Raw material: obsidian
Characteristics: Cotahuasi Valley – Valley of Volcanoes crossroads – *puna*; fresh and crushed peabbles, no outcrop, archaeological site (approx. 200 m²); two round structures of about 10 and 15 m
NAA: yes

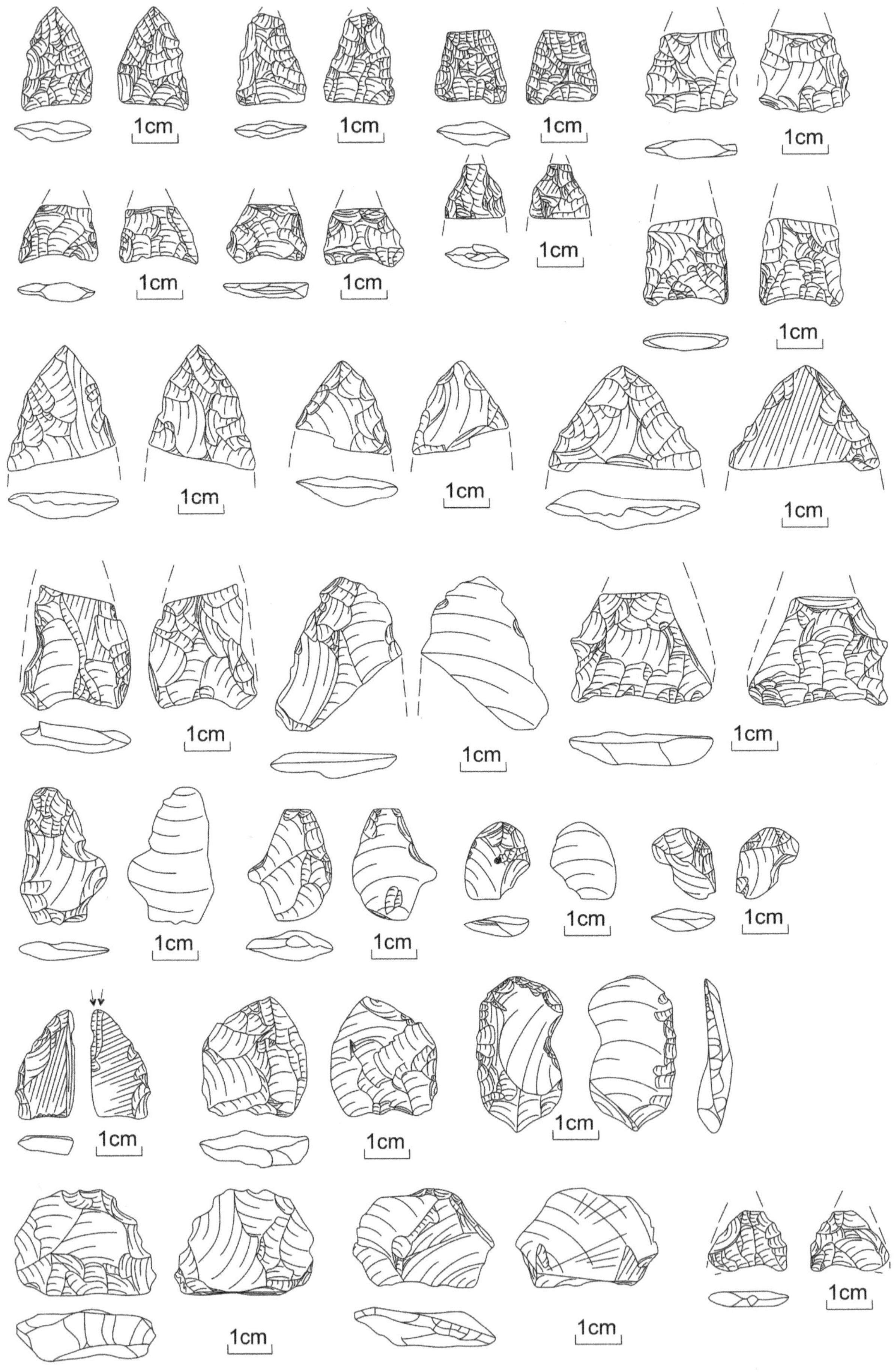

Fig. 41. Tools from O.11

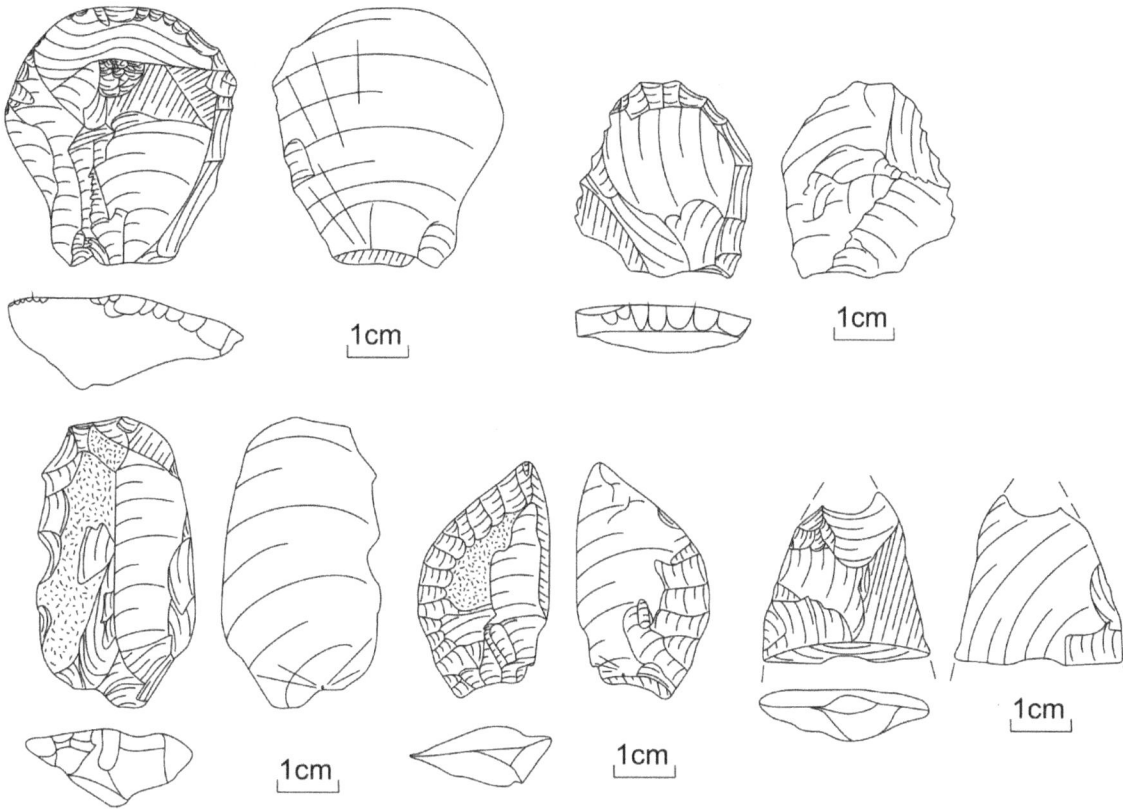

Fig. 42. Chalcedony tools from O11

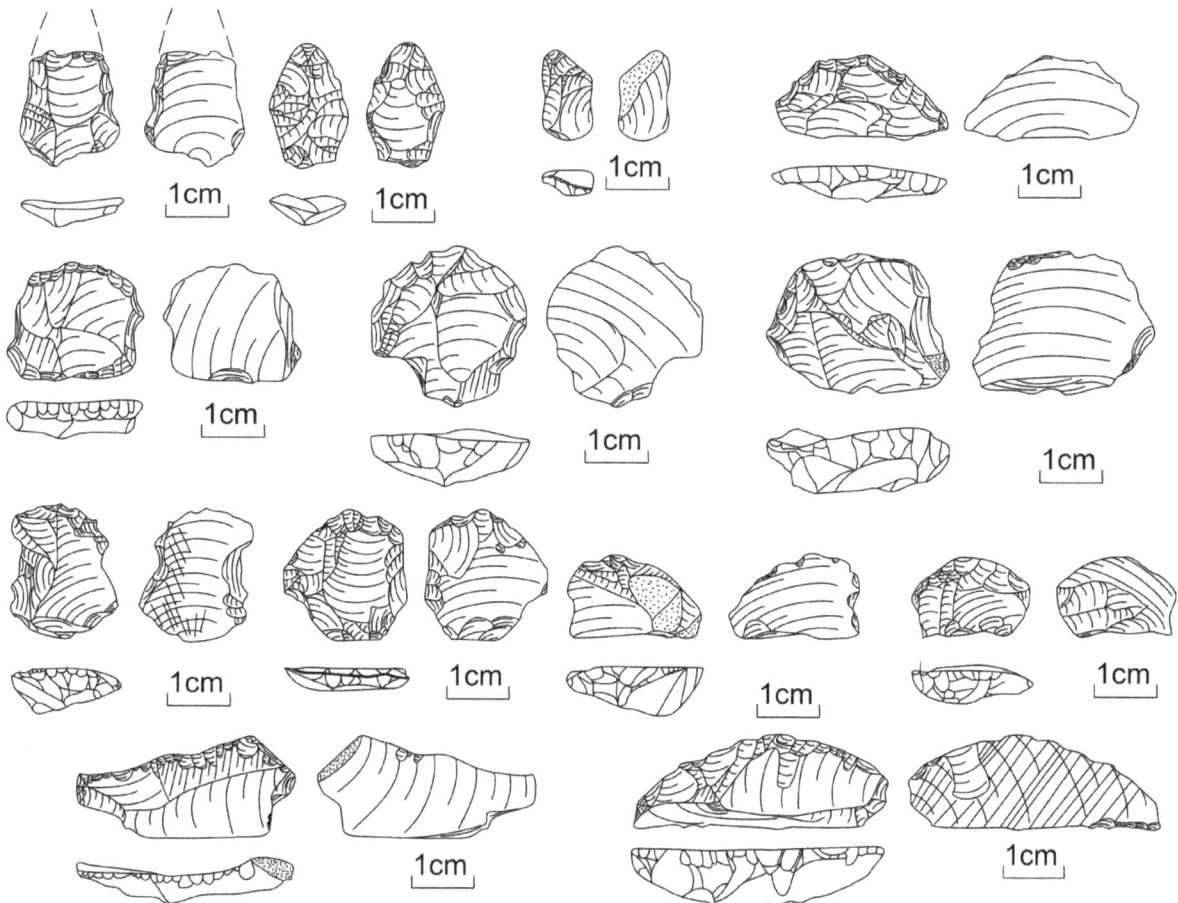

Fig. 43. Tools from O.12

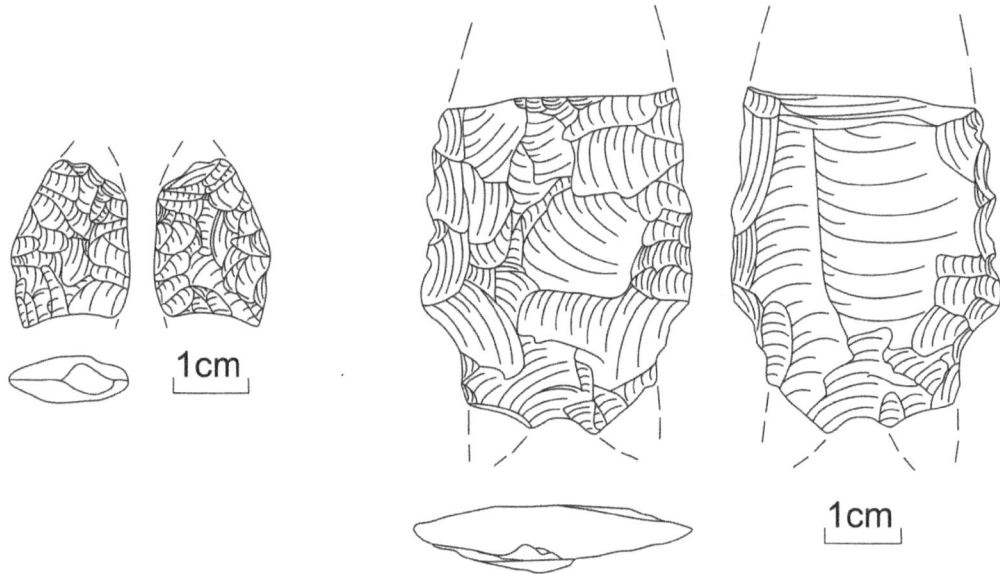

Fig. 44. Chalcedony and andesitic tools from O12

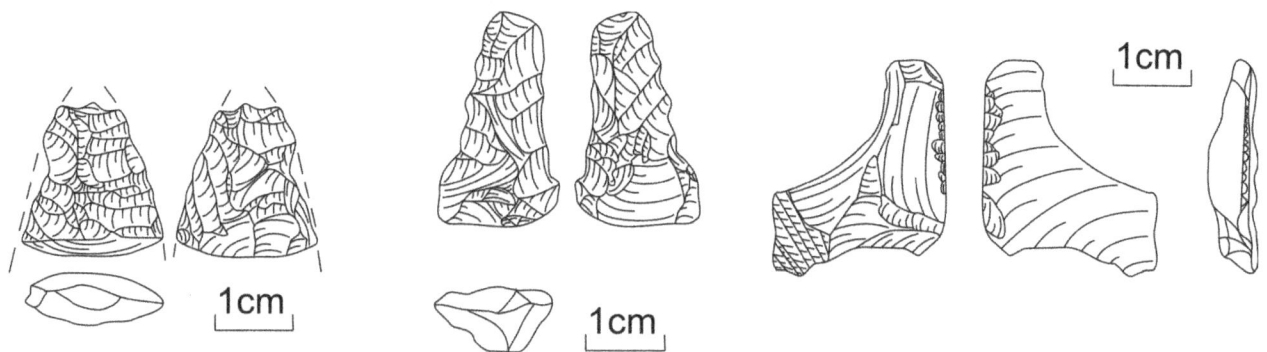

Fig. 45. Tools from D.01

Label: 1/05
Date: 30.06.2005
Geographical coordinates: 15°14'06'' S / 72°18'30'' W / 4150 m a.s.l.
Administrative location: Arequipa Departament, Castilla Province, Orcopampa District, Sarpane
Geomorphology: two planes in the middle of valley slope with excellent view on the valley
Field-collected samples:
 – flakes: obsidian 6, chalcedony 2
 – rock fragments: chalcedony 5
Raw material: obsidian; chalcedony: white, red, black
Characteristics: no outcrop, archaeological site (the majority of tools are collected in the school "museum" next to the site), the size of the site is very difficult to approximate beacause of contemporary use of terrain
NAA: yes (for obsidian)

Label: 4/05
Date: 30.06.2005
Geographical coordinates: 15°14'15'' S / 72°18'56'' W / 4030 m a.s.l.
Administrative location: Arequipa Departament, Castilla Province, Orcopampa District, 200 m N from Sarpane
Geomorphology: hill in the valley bottom

Field-collected samples
 – tools: 5 obsidian (3 projectil points fragments, denticulated tool, retouched flake; Fig. 46)
 – flakes: obsidian 10, chalcedony 1
Raw material: obsidian; white chalcedony
Characteristics: no outcrop, archaeological site, so called Ciminterio Sarpane and at the same time contemporary cemetary; obsidian tools and flakes are visible on the ground and are usually excavated during funeral ceremonies (the majority of them are collected in the Sarpane school "museum" – Fig. 34); there are some animal bones, the size of the site is very difficult to approximate beacause of contemporary use of terrain
NAA: yes (for obsidian)

Label: 5/05
Date: 01.07.2005
Geographical coordinates: quadrilateral 15°17'45'' S / 72°23'07'' W – 15°17'40'' S / 72°22'45'' W – 15°17'04'' S / 72°22'25'' W – 15°17'13'' S / 72°23'11'' W; 3928–4122 m a.s.l.
Administrative location: Arequipa Departament, Castilla Province, Chilcaymarca District
Geomorphology: the mouth of the side valley, small promontory on colluvial and alluvial sediments
Field-collected samples:
 – tools: 4 obsidian (4 projectil points and fragments; Fig. 47)

38

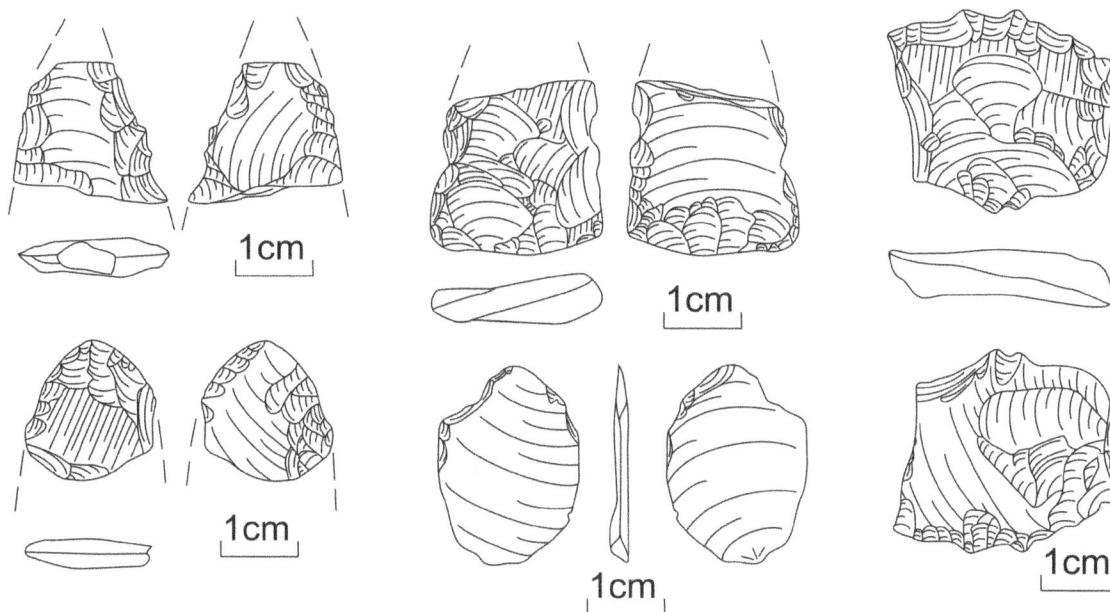

Fig. 46. Tools from 4/05

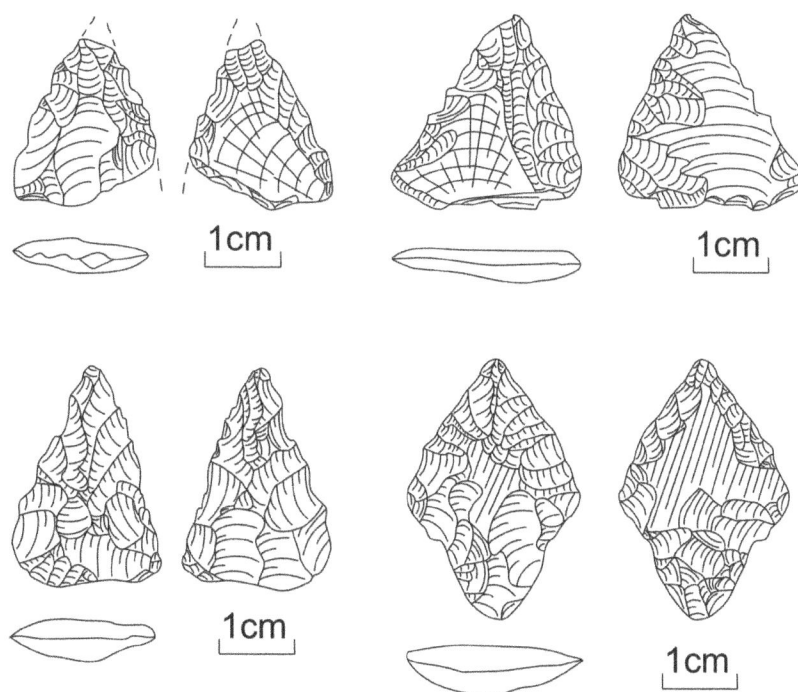

Fig. 47 Tools from 5/05

– flakes: obsidian 13, chalcedony 3
– rock fragments: obsidian 4, chalcedony 14
Raw material: obsidian; chalcedony: white, honey yellow, red, black
Characteristics: no outcrop, archaeological site (or sites?) in Chilcaymarca village and in its neighbourhood
NAA: yes (for obsidian)

Label: P1
Date: 02.07.2005
Geographical coordinates: 15°14'15'' S / 72°29'10'' W / 4800 m a.s.l.
Administrative location: Arequipa Departament, Castilla Prov-

ince, Chilcaymarca District
Geomorphology: big inter-mountain plateau
Field-collected samples
– tools: 1 obsidian (end-scraper; Fig. 48)
– flakes: obsidian 2, chalcedony 2
– rock fragments: chalcedony 2
Raw material: obsidian; chalcedony: gray, beige, white
Characteristics: no outcrop, archaeological site (or sites?) on the Pampa Lluliusha, approx. 150 m^2
NAA: yes (for obsidian)

Label: P2-3
Date: 02.07.2005

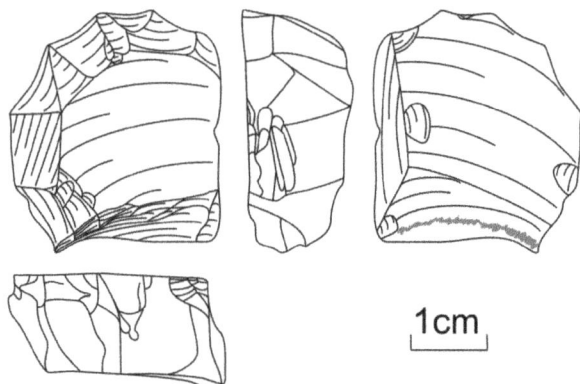

Fig. 48. Tool from P1

Geographical coordinates: 15°14'58'' S – 15°15'27'' S / 72°29'10'' W – 72°29'18'' W / 4750–4700 m a.s.l.
Administrative location: Arequipa Departament, Castilla Province, Chilcaymarca District
Geomorphology: big inter-mountain plateau
Field-collected samples:
   – tools: 7 (5 projectil points and fragments, end-scraper, denticulated tool; Fig. 47)
   – flakes: 2
   – rock fragments: 2
Raw material: obsidian
Characteristics: no outcrop, archaeological site (or sites?) on the Pampa Lluliusha
NAA: yes

Label: P4
Date: 02.07.2005
Geographical coordinates: 15°16'00'' S / 72°29'46'' W / 4500 m a.s.l.
Administrative location: Arequipa Departament, Castilla Province, Chilcaymarca District

Geomorphology: intermountain valley, marshy land between two streams
Field-collected samples:
   – tools: 3 obsidian (projectile point fragment, 2 retouched flakes; Fig. 50)
   – flakes: obsidian 14, chalcedony 5
   – rock fragments: obsidian 6, chalcedony 9
Raw material: obsidian black and red; chalcedony: white, yellow, brown, red
Characteristics: no outcrop, archaeological site (or sites?) near so called Ruinas, approx. 200 m²
NAA: yes (for obsidian)

Label: P5
Date: 02.07.2005
Geographical coordinates: 15°15'38'' S / 72°29'48'' W / 4500 m a.s.l.
Administrative location: Arequipa Departament, Castilla Province, Chilcaymarca District
Geomorphology: intermountain valley, marshy land between two streams
Field-collected samples:
   – tools: 2 obsidian (end-scraper, *piece esquille*; Fig. 51)
   – flakes: obsidian 1, chalcedony 1
   – rock fragments: chalcedony 2
Raw material: obsidian; chalcedony: white and brown
Characteristics: no outcrop, archaeological site (or sites?) near so called Ruinas, approx. 100 m²
NAA: no

Label: P6
Date: 02.07.2005
Geographical coordinates: 15°16'15'' S / 72°30'15'' W / 4400 m a.s.l.
Administrative location: Arequipa Departament, Castilla Province, Chilcaymarca District
Geomorphology: intermountain valley, marshy land between two streams

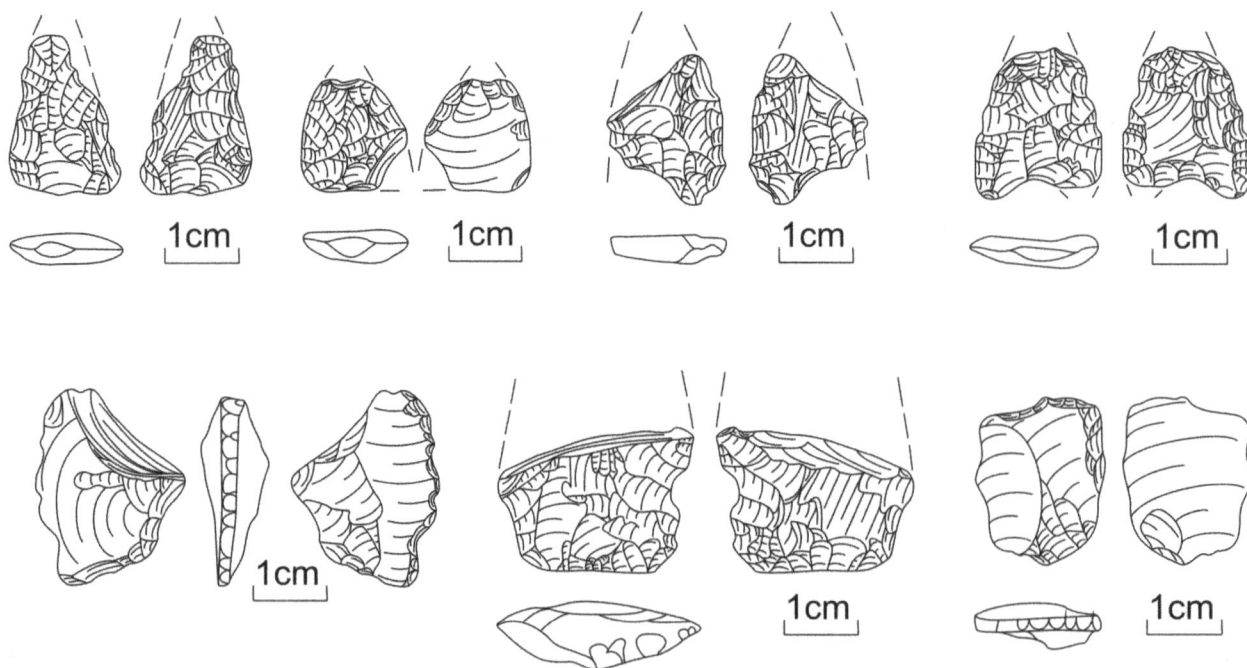

Fig. 49. Tools from P2-3

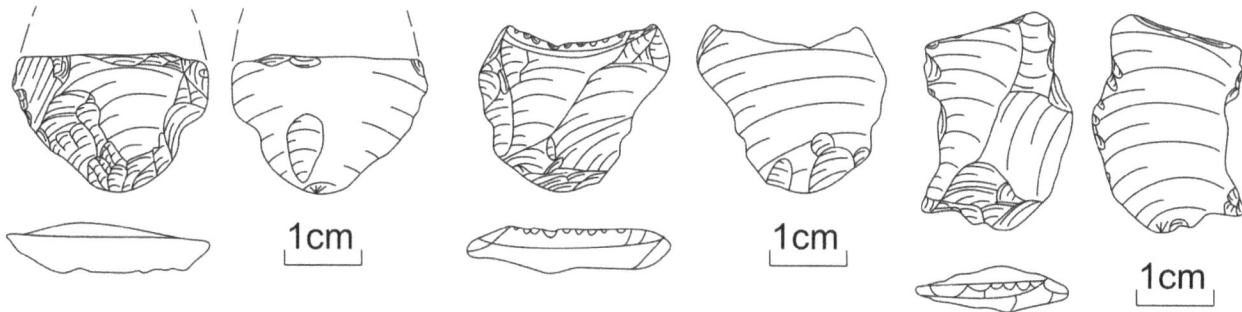

Fig. 50. Tools from P4

Field-collected samples:
– tools: 3 (projectil point, 2 perforators (one made on the projectil point, one with denticulate retouch of sides); Fig. 52)
– flakes: 4
Raw material: obsidian
Characteristics: no outcrop, archaeological site (or sites?) near so called Ruinas, approx. 100 m²
NAA: no

Label: P7
Date: 02.07.2005
Geographical coordinates: 15°11'37'' S / 72°30'25'' W / 4900 m a.s.l.
Administrative location: Arequipa Departament, Castilla Province, Chilcaymarca District
Geomorphology: intermountain valley
Field-collected samples:
– core (Fig. 53)
– tools: (retouched flake)
Raw material: obsidian
Characteristics: no outcrop, archaeological site (or sites?) near Poracota Mine
NAA: yes

Label: P10
Date: 03.07.2005
Geographical coordinates: 15°12'02'' S / 72°29'15'' W / 4400 m a.s.l.
Administrative location: Arequipa Departament, Castilla Province, Chilcaymarca District, Laguna Incamisa
Geomorphology: intermountain valley, marshy land

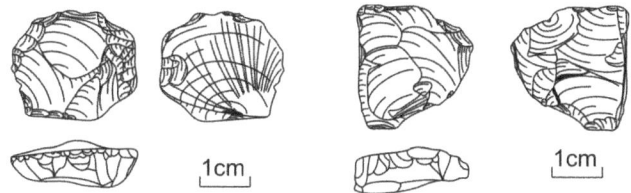

Fig. 51. Tools from P5

Field-collected samples:
– tools: 1 obsidian (projectil point; Fig. 54)
– rock fragments: 2
Raw material: obsidian; chalcedony: white, red
Characteristics: no outcrop, loose finding, no context
NAA: no

Label: P11
Date: 03.07.2005
Geographical coordinates: 15°11'27'' S / 72°29'48'' W / 4500 m a.s.l.
Administrative location: Arequipa Departament, Castilla Province, Chilcaymarca District, Cerro Cachipascana
Geomorphology: intermountain valley, mouth of the side gorge
Field-collected samples:
– tools: 1 (burin; Fig. 55)
Raw material: obsidian
Characteristics: no outcrop, loose finding, no context
NAA: no

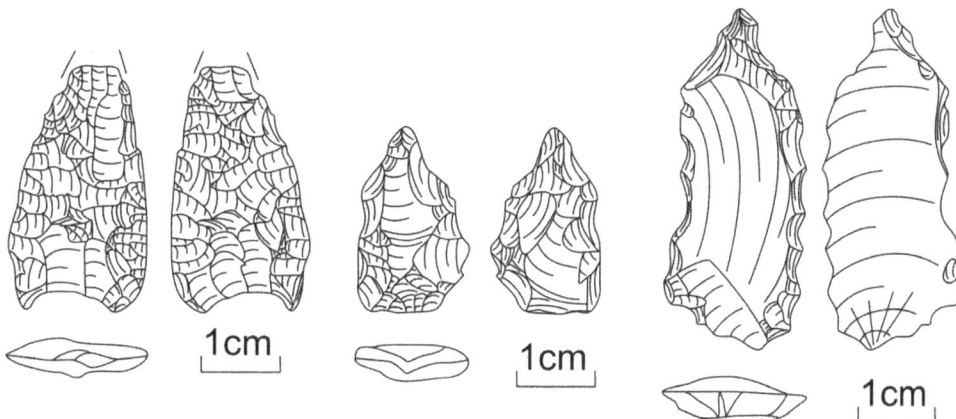

Fig. 52. Tools from P6

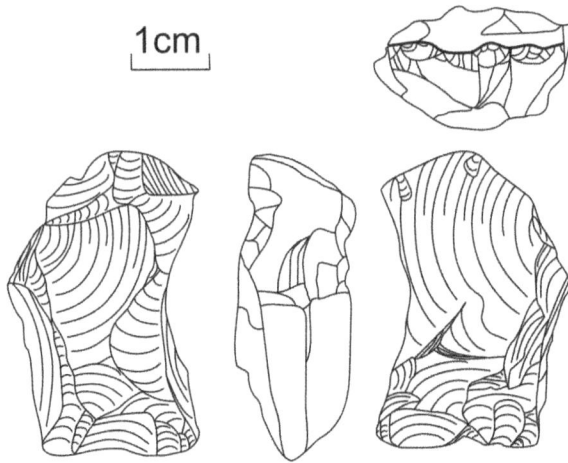

Fig. 53. Core from P7

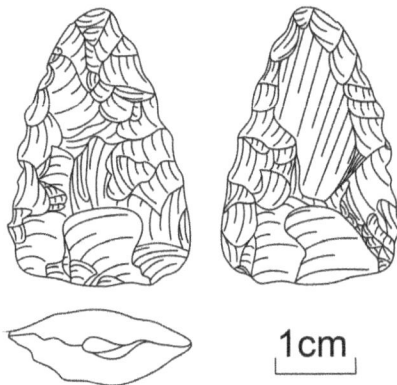

Fig. 54. Tool from P10

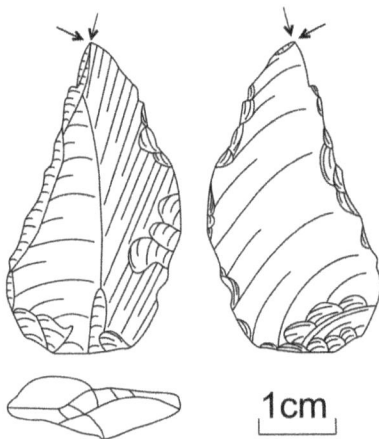

Fig. 55. Tool from P11

Label: P12
Date: 03.07.2005
Geographical coordinates: 15°09'42'' S – 15°09'37'' S / 72°31'32'' W – 72°31'40'' W / 4600–4640 m a.s.l.
Admirnistrative location: Arequipa Departament, Castilla Province, Chilcaymarca District, Cerro Cachipascana NE
Geomorphology: intermountain valley, marshy land, plaine
Field-collected samples:

– tools: 6 obsidian (projectil point and fragment, side-scraper, perforator, 2 retouched flakes; Fig. 56)
– flakes: obsidian 6, chalcedony 2
– rock fragments: obsidian 2
Raw material: obsidian; chalcedony: black, red
Characteristics: no outcrop, archaeological site, approx. 200 m^2
NAA: yes (for obsidian)

Label: P13
Date: 03.07.2005
Geographical coordinates: 15°09'28'' S / 72°31'40'' W / 4680 m a.s.l.
Administrative location: Arequipa Departament, Castilla Province, Chilcaymarca District, Quebrada Caliente-Quebrada Mal Aire
Geomorphology: gully mouth, stream terrace
Field-collected samples:
– flakes: 2
Raw material: chalcedony: black, brown
Characteristics: no outcrop
NAA: no

Label: P14
Date: 03.07.2005
Geographical coordinates: 15°09'36'' S / 72°31'34'' W / 4680 m a.s.l.
Administrative location: Arequipa Departament, Castilla Province, Chilcaymarca District, Quebrada Caliente
Geomorphology: gully mouth, plain above the stream
Field-collected samples:
– core: 1 chalcedony core (Fig. 58)
– tools: 1 obsidian (projectil point; Fig. 57)
– flakes: chalcedony 2
– rock fragments: chalcedony 1
Raw material: obsidian; chalcedony: black, brown; andesitic lava of the Andagua Formation
Characteristics: no outcrop, archaeological site, approx. 250 m^2
NAA: no

Label: U1
Date: 05.07.2005
Geographical coordinates: 15°13'30'' S / 72°23'34'' W / 3900 m a.s.l.
Administrative location: Arequipa Departament, Condesuyos Province, Cayarani District, Cuchurancho
Geomorphology: intermountain valley
Field-collected samples:
– flakes: obsidian 2, chalcedony 1
– rock fragments: obsidian 2
Raw material: obsidian; white chalcedony
Characteristics: no outcrop, loose findings in contemporary village
NAA: yes (for obsidian)

Label: W2
Date: 07.07.2005
Geographical coordinates: 15°09'22'' S – 15°09'11'' S / 72°28'40'' W – 72°28'35'' W / 4380–4420 m a.s.l.
Administrative location: Arequipa Departament, Castilla Province, Chilcaymarca District, Cerro Sayacata
Geomorphology: hill slope of the Alpabamba Formation, *puna* zone
Field-collected samples:
– flakes: obsidian 15, chalcedony 1
– rock fragments: obsidian 11
Raw material: obsidian; red-white chalcedony

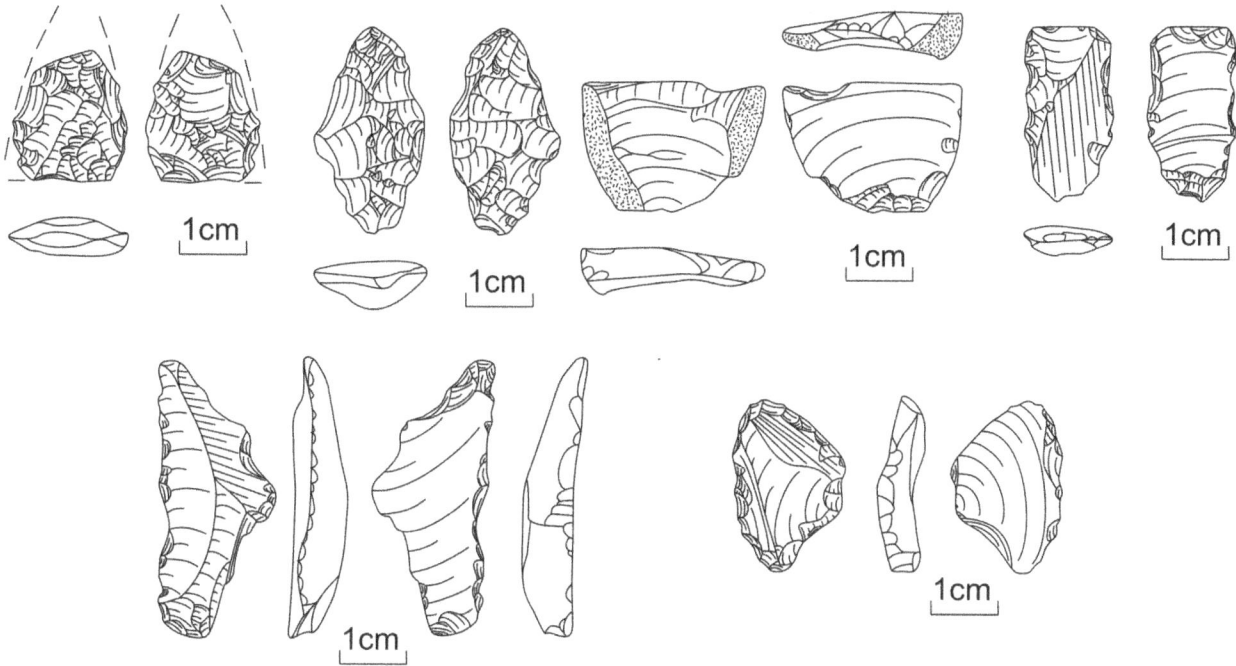

Fig. 56. Tools from P12

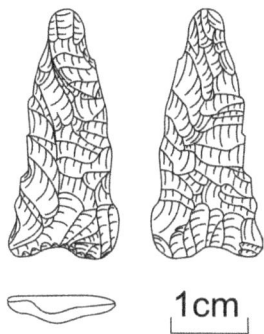

Fig. 57. Tool from P14

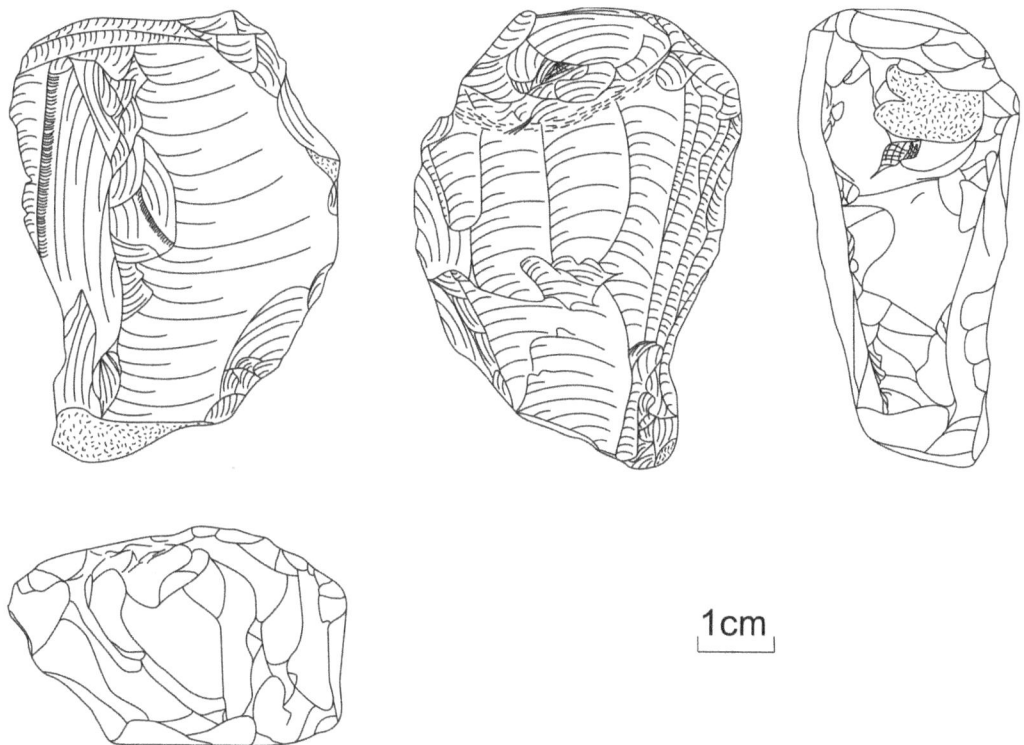

Fig. 58. Chalcedony core from P14

Characteristics: outcrop, archaeological site (?), approx. 250 m^2
NAA: yes (for obsidian)

Label: W3
Date: 07.07.2005
Geographical coordinates: 15°09'46'' S / 72°27'57'' W / 4400 m a.s.l.
Administrative location: Arequipa Departament, Castilla Province, Chilcaymarca District

Geomorphology: small elevations on plateau
Field-collected samples:
   – tools: 3 (2 projectil points fragments, double convergent side-scraper; Fig. 59)
   – flakes: 2
Raw material: obsidian
Characteristics: no outcrop, archaeological site, approx. 150 m^2
NAA: no

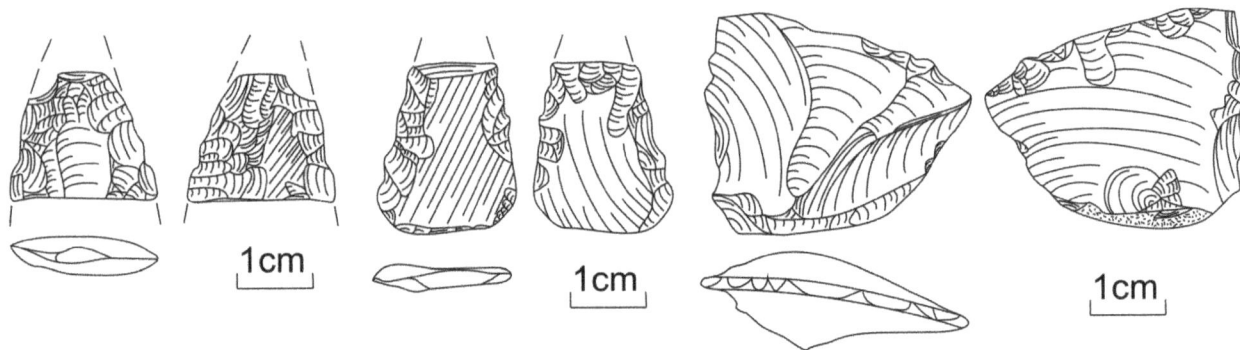

Fig. 59.   Tools from W3

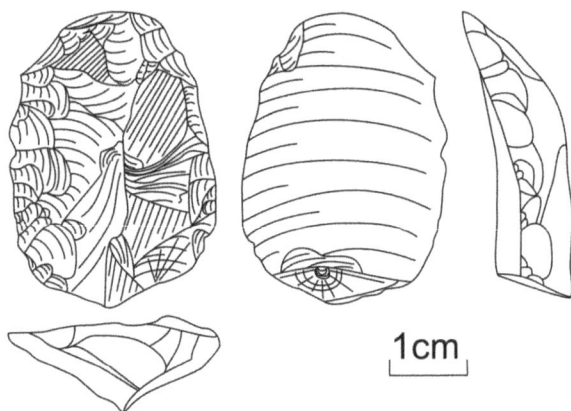

Fig. 60.   Tool from W4

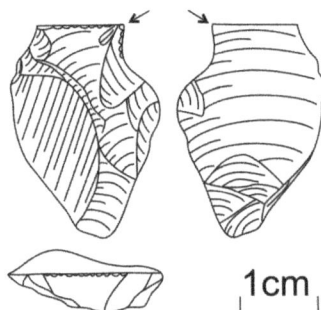

Fig. 61.   Tool from W5

Label: W4
Date: 07.07.2005
Geographical coordinates: 15°08'20'' S / 72°26'23'' W / 4420 m a.s.l.
Administrative location: Arequipa Departament, Castilla Province, Chilcaymarca District, Quebrada Paco
Geomorphology: small gullies, sources of Umachulco River
Field-collected samples:
     – tools: 1 (end-scraper on side-scraper; Fig. 60)
     – flakes: 2
Raw material: obsidian
Characteristics: no outcrop, loose findings
NAA: no

Label: W5
Date: 08.07.2005
Geographical coordinates: 15°08'07'' S / 72°26'20'' W / 4500 m a.s.l.
Administrative location: Arequipa Departament, Condesuyos Province, Cayarani District
Geomorphology: small gullies, sources of Umachulco river
Field-collected samples:
     – tools: 1 obsidian (burin; Fig. 61) and 3 chalcedony
     (2 end-scrapers, knife; Fig. 62)
     – flakes: obsidian 7, chalcedony 2
Raw material: obsidian black and red; chalcedon: white, brown
Characteristics: no outcrop, archaeological site, approx. 250 m²
NAA: yes (for obsidian)

Label: W6-7
Date: 08.07.2005
Geographical coordinates: 15°07'46'' S – 15°07'48'' S / 72°25'53'' W – 72°25'23'' W / 4530 m a.s.l.
Administrative location: Arequipa Departament, Condesuyos Province, Cayarani District
Geomorphology: small gullies, sources of Umachulco river

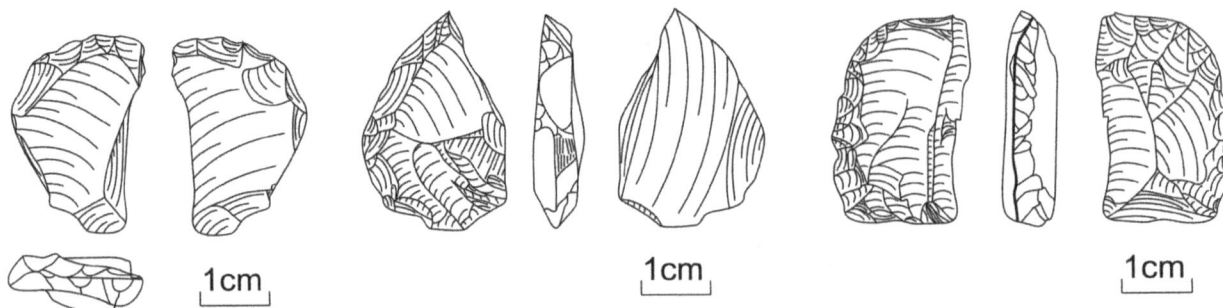

Fig. 62.   Chalcedony tools from W5

Field-collected samples:
  – tools: 1 obsidian (projectil point; Fig. 63)
  – flakes: obsidian 6, chalcedony 4
  – rock fragments: obsidian 2
Raw material: obsidian; red chalcedony; andesitic lava of Andagua Formation
Characteristics: no outcrop, archaeological site (?), approx. 150 m^2
NAA: yes (for obsidian)

Label: W8
Date: 08.07.2005
Geographical coordinates: 15°07'40'' S / 72°25'36'' W / 4520 m a.s.l.
Administrative location: Arequipa Departament, Condesuyos Province, Cayarani District, Pampa Jararanca

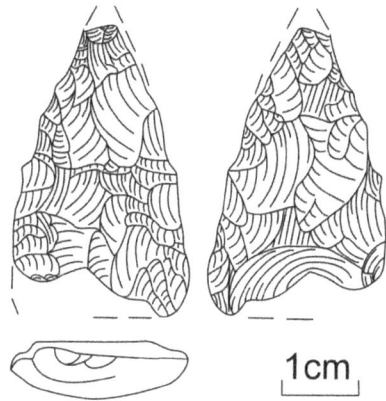

Fig. 63.   Tool from W6-7

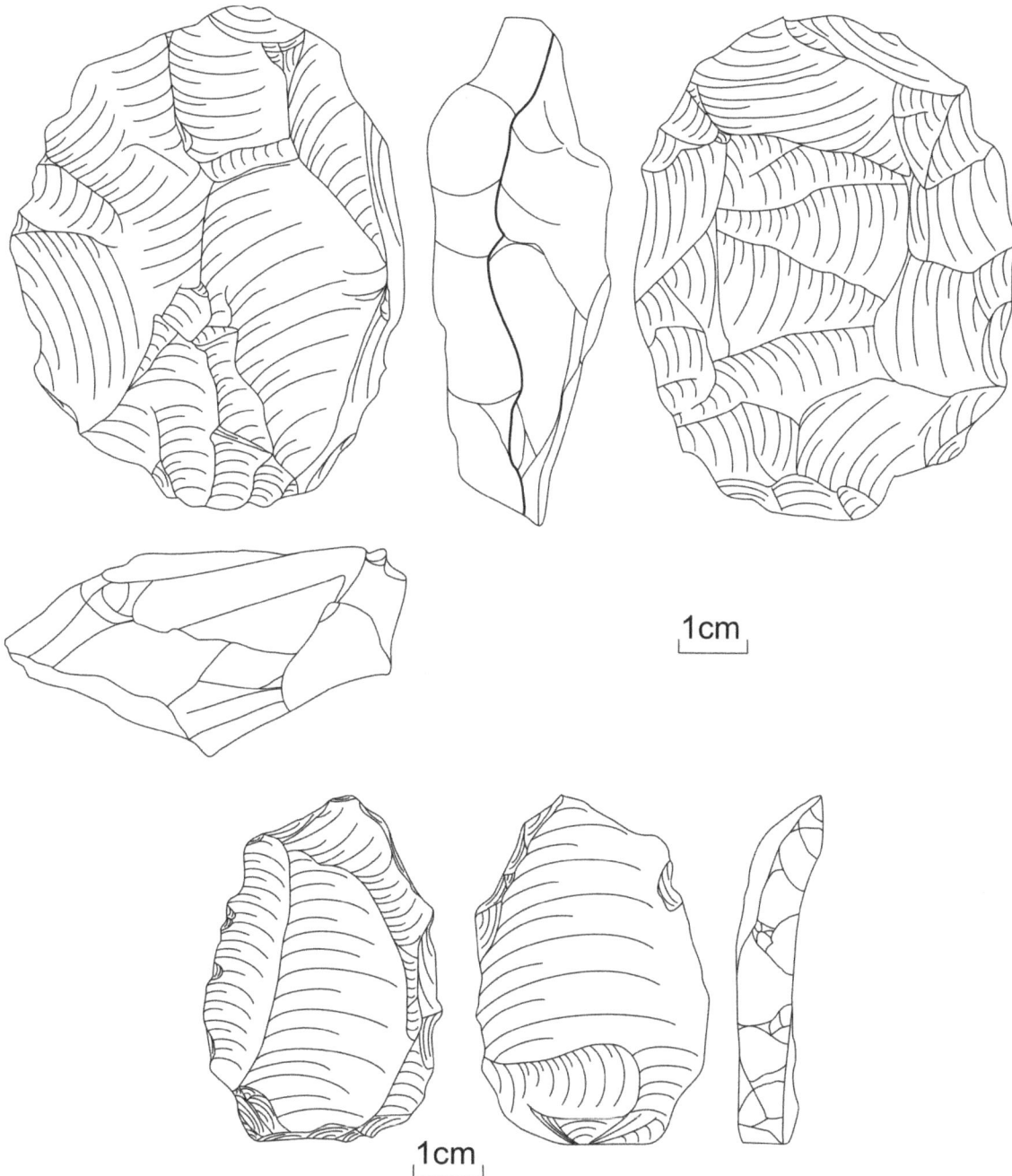

Fig. 64.   Core and andesitic tool from W8.

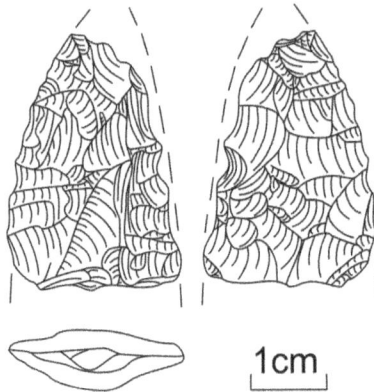

Fig. 65. Tool from W11-12.

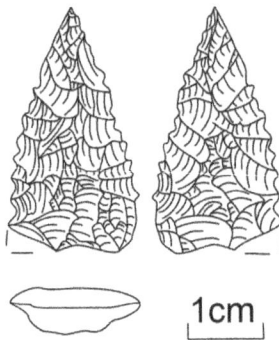

Fig. 66. Tool from W15.

Geomorphology: plateau
Field-collected samples:
 – core: 1 (Fig. 64)
 – tool: 1 (backed piece on flake; Fig. 64)
 – flakes: 1
Raw material: andesitic lava
Characteristics: local andesitic lava, archaeological site (two stone circles)
NAA: no

Label: W9
Date: 08.07.2005
Geographical coordinates: 15°06'59'' S / 72°26'16'' W / 4500 m a.s.l.
Administrative location: Arequipa Departament, Condesuyos Province, Cayarani District, Pampa Jararanca
Geomorphology: promontory on the plateau river
Field-collected samples:
– flakes: obsidian 7, chalcedony 4
– rock fragments: chalcedony 2
Raw material: obsidian black and red; chalcedony: white, brown
Characteristics: no outcrop, archaeological site, approx. 200 m²
NAA: no

Label: W11-12
Date: 08.07.2005
Geographical coordinates: 15°05'41'' S – 15°06'08'' S / 72°27'36'' W – 72°27'21'' W / 4650 m a.s.l.
Administrative location: Arequipa Departament, Condesuyos Province, Cayarani District, Quebrada Ushpa Corral
Geomorphology: intermountain valley, hills' slopes
Field-collected samples:
 – tools: 1 (projectil point; Fig. 65)

 – flakes: 2
 – rock fragments: 6
Raw material: obsidian
Characteristics: outcrop
NAA: yes

Label: W14
Date: 09.07.2005
Geographical coordinates: 15°07'38'' S / 72°24'55'' W / 4470 m a.s.l.
Administrative location: Arequipa Departament, Condesuyos Province, Cayarani District, Pampa Jararanca
Geomorphology: plateau
Field-collected samples:
 – flakes: 5
 – rock fragments: 2
Raw material: obsidian
Characteristics: no outcrop, archaeological site (?), approx. 150 m²
NAA: yes

Label: W15
Date: 09.07.2005
Geographical coordinates: 15°09'30'' S / 72°22'54'' W / 4470 m a.s.l.
Administrative location: Arequipa Departament, Condesuyos Province, Cayarani District, Pampa Jararanca-Cerro Chanchaclla
Geomorphology: plateau
Field-collected samples:
 – tools: 1 (projectil point; Fig. 66)
 – flakes: 4
Raw material: obsidian
Characteristics: no outcrop, archaeological site (?)
NAA: yes

Label: V2
Date: 13.07.2005
Geographical coordinates: 15°09'42'' S – 15°09'06'' S / 72°26'52'' W – 72°26'24'' W / 4470 m a.s.l.
Administrative location: Arequipa Departament, Castilla Province, Chilcaymarca District, Quebrada Paco
Geomorphology: upper part of the gully, sources of Umachulco river
Field-collected samples:
 – tools: 2 obsidian (projectile point fragment, asymmetrical perforator; Fig. 67)
 – flakes: obsidian 7, chalcedony 3
 – rock fragments: obsidian 3
Raw material: obsidian black and red; chalcedony: white, yellow
Characteristics: no outcrop, archaeological site, approx. 150 m²
NAA: yes (for obsidian)

Label: V3
Date: 13.07.2005
Geographical coordinates: 15°08'34'' S / 72°26'07'' W / 4490 m a.s.l.
Administrative location: Arequipa Departament, Castilla Province, Chilcaymarca District, Quebrada Paco
Geomorphology: lower part of the gully, sources of the Umachulco river
Field-collected samples:
 – tools: 1 obsidian (półtylczak; Fig. 68) and 1 chalcedony (retouched flake; Fig. 69)
 – flakes: obsidian 4, chalcedony 2
 – rock fragments: chalcedony 3

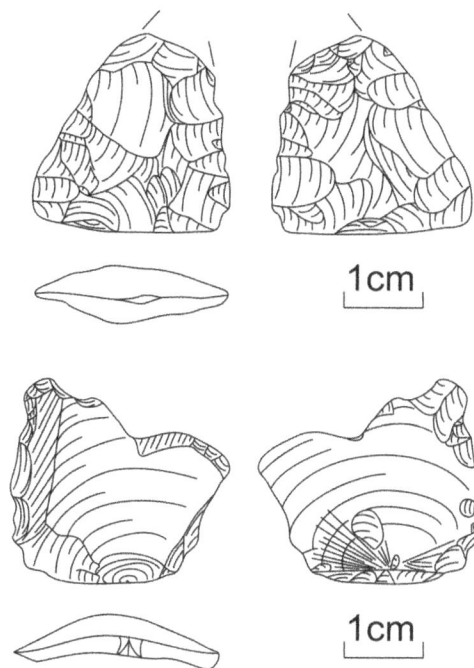

Fig. 67. Tools from V2.

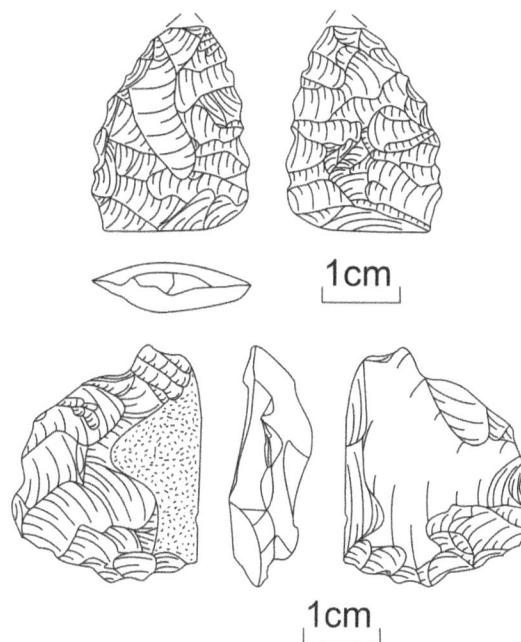

Fig. 68. Tool from V3

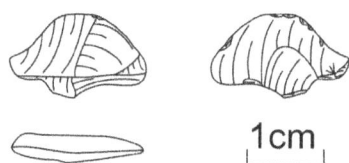

Fig. 69. Retouched chalcedony flake from V3

Raw material: obsidian; chalcedony: white, red
Characteristics: no outcrop, archaeological site, stone "wall" from the site of the river and gully mouth, approx. 200 m^2
NAA: yes (for obsidian)

Label: V4
Date: 14.07.2005
Geographical coordinates: 15°08'34'' S / 72°26'07'' W / 4490 m a.s.l.
Administrative location: Arequipa Departament, Condesuyos Province, Cayarani District, Sonco Palca
Geomorphology: bottom of the intermountain valley
Field-collected samples:
  – tools: 2 (projectil point, tool with initial retouche; Fig. 70)
  – flakes: 3
  – rock fragments: 2

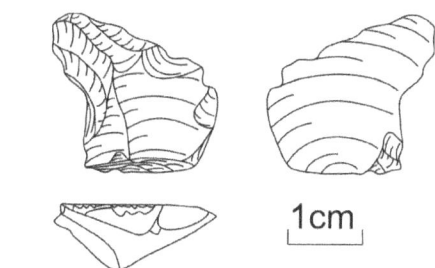

Fig. 70. Tools from V4.

Raw material: obsidian
Characteristics: no outcrop, archaeological site, approx. 200 m^2
NAA: yes

Label: V8
Date: 15.07.2005
Geographical coordinates: 15°06'31'' S / 72°22'10'' W / 4570 m a.s.l.
Administrative location: Arequipa Departament, Condesuyos Province, Cayarani District, Pabellon
Geomorphology: mountain slope above the plain where three intermountain valleys converge
Field-collected samples:
  – tools: 2 obsidian (projectile point fragment, retouched flake; Fig. 71)
  – flakes: obsidian 7, chalcedony 2
Raw material: obsidian; chalcedony: white, red
Characteristics: no outcrop, archaeological site, approx. 200 m^2
NAA: yes (for obsidian)

Label: V9 (as W15)
Date: 16.07.2005
Geographical coordinates: 15°09'46'' S / 72°22'53'' W / 4500 m a.s.l.
Administrative location: Arequipa Departament, Condesuyos Province, Cayarani District, Pampa Jararanca-Cerro Chanchaclla
Geomorphology: plateau
Field-collected samples:
  – tools: 2 obsidian (projectil point fragment, *raclette*; Fig. 72)
  – flakes: obsidian 4, chalcedony 2
Raw material: obsidian; white chalcedony
Characteristics: no outcrop, archaeological site
NAA: no

Label: PJ
Date: 07–09.07.2005
Geographical coordinates: –
Administrative location: Arequipa Departament, Condesuyos

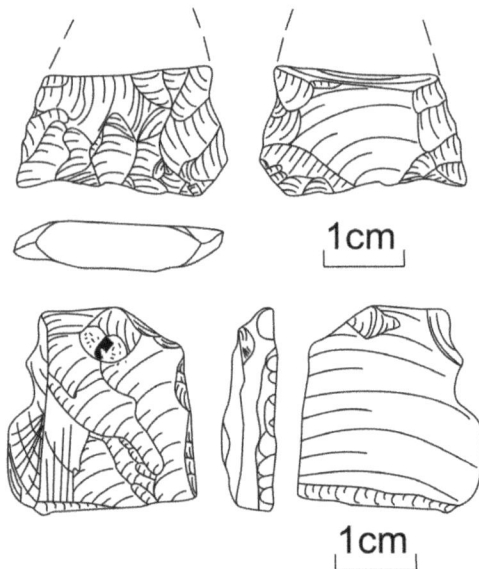

Fig. 71. Tools from V8

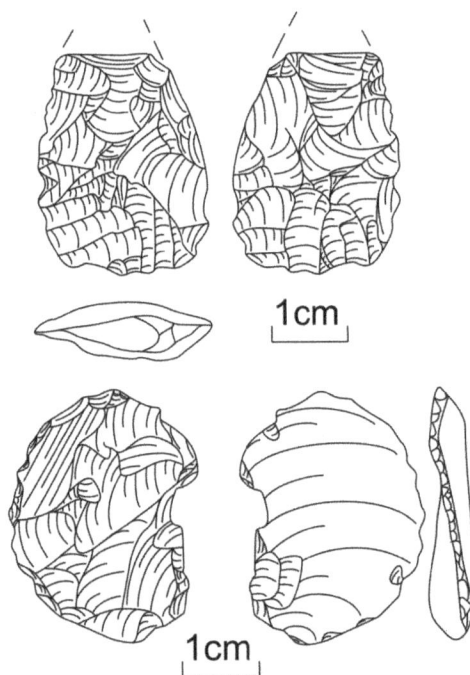

Fig. 72. Tools from V9.

Province, Cayarani District, Pampa Jararanca
Geomorphology: plateau
Field-collected samples:
 – tools: 3 obsidian (2 end-scrapers, retouched flake; Fig. 73)
 – flakes: obsidian 3, chalcedony 2
 – rock fragments: chalcedony 1
Raw material: obsidian; chalcedony: white, brown
Characteristics: no outcrop, loose findings
NAA: no

Label: SP-P
Date: 15.07.2005
Geographical coordinates: –
Administrative location: Arequipa Departament, Condesuyos

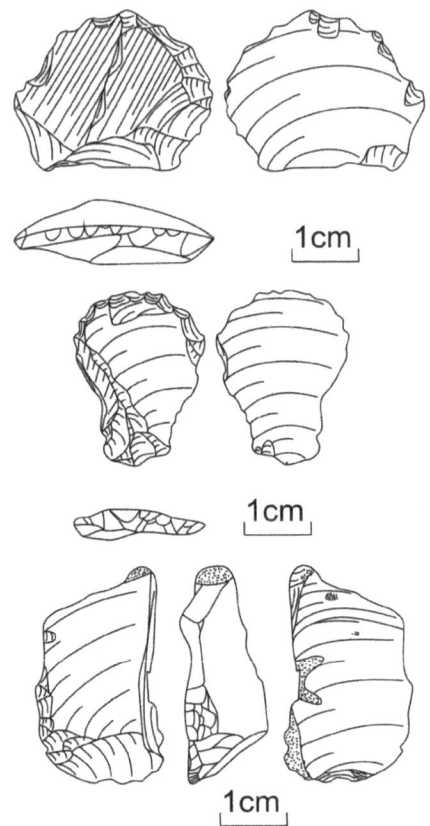

Fig. 73. Tools from PJ

Province, Cayarani District, Rio Soncopalca
Geomorphology: intermountain valley
Field-collected samples:
 – tools: 2 obsidian (projectile point fragment, *raclette*; Fig. 74)
 – flakes: obsidian 7, chalcedony 1
 – rock fragments: obsidian 4, chalcedony 1
Raw material: obsidian; white chalcedony; andesitic lava of Andagua Formation
Characteristics: no outcrop, loose findings
NAA: no

Label: OR
Date: 23.07.2005
Geographical coordinates: 15°14'03'' S / 72°17'12'' W / 3950 m a.s.l.
Administrative location: Arequipa Departament, Castilla Province, Orcopampa District, Orcopampa
Geomorphology: –
Field-collected samples:
 – flakes: 1
 – rock fragments: 3
Raw material: obsidian
Characteristics: no outcrop, loose findings from contemporary city
NAA: yes

List of raw materials outcrops in the Valle de los Volcanes (see Map)

Label: 2
Date: 15.07.2004
Geographical coordinates: 15°28'54'' S / 72°20'11'' W / 3480 m a.s.l.

Administrative location: Arequipa Departament, Castilla Province, Andagua District
Geomorphology: western, steep slope of the river valley-canyon
Field-collected samples:
  – rock fragments: 1
Raw material: green "obsidian"
Characteristics: neighbourhood of the hanging bridge on Andagua river; pojedyncze loose finding, no context, no outcrop
NAA: yes

Label: 3-4
Date: 15.07.2004
Geographical coordinates: 15°28'37'' S / 72°19'23'' W / 3450–3400 m a.s.l.
Administrative location: Arequipa Departament, Castilla Province, Andagua District, Site Tauca
Geomorphology: lava stream in form of the promontory above river valley
Field-collected samples:
  – rock fragments: 2
Raw material: andesitic lava of Andagua Formation
Characteristics: local raw materials from the pre-Inca cementery site (nore precise chronology unknown)
NAA: no

Label: O.7
Date: 20.07.2004
Geographical coordinates: 15°12'59'' S / 72°19'28'' W / 4000 m a.s.l.
Administrative location: Arequipa Departament, Castilla Province, Orcopampa District, Paracapujyo site
Geomorphology: valley slope
Field-collected samples:
  – rock fragments: 4
Raw material: chalcedony: white, gray, honey yellow, green
Characteristics: chalcedony vein in the ignimbrites
NAA: no

Label: 2/05
Date: 30.06.2005
Geographical coordinates: 15°14'05'' S / 72°17'11'' W / 4280 m a.s.l.
Administrative location: Arequipa Departament, Castilla Province, Orcopampa District, Suyto Occo
Geomorphology: upper part of the side crest
Field-collected samples:
  – rock fragments: 4
Raw material: chalcedony: black, black white spotted
Characteristics: outcrop of the silicified vein
NAA: no

Label: 3/05
Date: 30.06.2005
Geographical coordinates: 15°13'50'' S / 72°16'44'' W – 72°16'43'' W / 4220–4277 m a.s.l.
Administrative location: Arequipa Departament, Castilla Province, Orcopampa District, Utco
Geomorphology: upper part of the crest, rock mushrooms and steep walls of the small gully
Field-collected samples:
  – flakes: 5
  – rock fragments: 15
Raw material: chalcedony: white, beige, black, red, colourless
Characteristics: outcrop, chalcedony vein in the tuffites
NAA: no

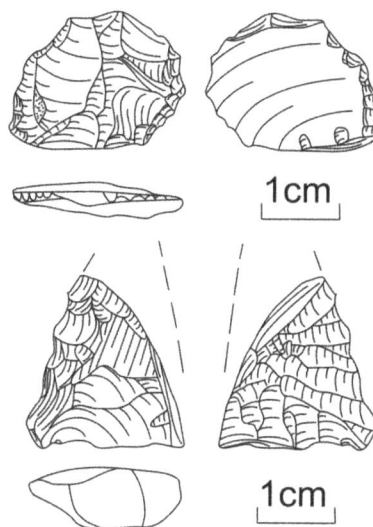

Fig. 74. Tools from SP-P

Label: P15
Date: 03.07.2005
Geographical coordinates: 15°09'56'' S / 72°31'41'' W / 4690 m a.s.l.
Administrative location: Arequipa Departament, Castilla Province, Chilcaymarca District
Geomorphology: valley slope
Field-collected samples:
  – rock fragments: 4
Raw material: chalcedony: black, brown
Characteristics: outcrop
NAA: no

Label: W1
Date: 07.07.2005
Geographical coordinates: 15°09'08'' S / 72°27'53'' W / 4350 m a.s.l.
Administrative location: Arequipa Departament, Castilla Province, Chilcaymarca District, Cerro Huancahuire
Geomorphology: hill slope of Alpabamba Formation, *puna* zone
Field-collected samples:
  – flakes: 2 (in the *puna* zone)
  – rock fragments: 9
Raw material: obsidian
Characteristics: outcrop, small peabbles
NAA: yes

Label: W10
Date: 08.07.2005
Geographical coordinates: 15°05'41'' S / 72°27'36'' W / 4650 m a.s.l.
Administrative location: Arequipa Departament, Condesuyos Province, Cayarani District, Mistisa Palca
Geomorphology: intermountain valley, hill slopes
Field-collected samples:
  – rock fragments: 2
Raw material: obsidian
Characteristics: outcrop
NAA: yes

Label: W13
Date: 08.07.2005
Geographical coordinates: 15°05'41'' S / 72°27'36'' W /

4655–4550 m a.s.l.
Administrative location: Arequipa Departament, Condesuyos Province, Cayarani District, Quebrada Ushpa Corral
Geomorphology: intermountain valley, hill slopes
Field-collected samples:
  – flakes: 2
  – rock fragments: 7
Raw material: obsidian
Characteristics: outcrop
NAA: yes

Label: V1
Date: 13.07.2005
Geographical coordinates: 15°09'58'' S / 72°27'42'' W / 4470 m a.s.l.
Administrative location: Arequipa Departament, Castilla Province, Chilcaymarca District, Paco
Geomorphology: mountain slope
Field-collected samples:
  – rock fragments: 1
Raw material: obsidian
Characteristics: no outcrop, loose finding
NAA: no

Label: V5-6
Date: 14.07.2005
Geographical coordinates: 15°03'05'' S – 15°03'08'' S / 72°23'38'' W – 72°23'37'' W / 4560–4530 m a.s.l.
Administrative location: Arequipa Departament, Condesuyos Province, Cayarani District, Quebrada Huañajahua
Geomorphology: slope of the intermountain valley
Field-collected samples:
  – rock fragments: 65
Raw material: obsidian
Characteristics: outcrops and colluvia
NAA: yes

Label: V7
Date: 14.07.2005
Geographical coordinates: 15°02'22'' S – 15°01'36'' S / 72°23'36'' W – 72°23'34'' W / 4560–4580 m a.s.l.
Administrative location: Arequipa Departament, Condesuyos Province, Cayarani District, Cerro Aljajahua
Geomorphology: slopes of the lava domes, covered with tiffites
Field-collected samples:
  – rock fragments: 25
Raw material: obsidian
Characteristics: outcrops and colluvia
NAA: yes

As seen in the material presented, projectile points and their fragments dominate (51 pieces) among items inventoried. Besides these, there have been found: end-scrapers (22), perforators (5), side-scrapers (4), denticulated tools (3), knives (3), burins (3), *pieces esquilles* (3), *raclettes* (2), backed piece on flake (1), truncated blade (1), tools with initial retouch (1) and retouched flakes (23). Additionally, 3 cores have been described. This gives a total number of 122 tools with respect to 506 flakes, or a relationship of 1:4.15. This very low indicator of flakes, however, ensues only in part from the real percent composition of artifacts on the sites that have been surveyed[36]. In large measure, it is a reflection of the intentional focus of attention on those objects which, due to their character, are: firstly – most often col-

lected by chance discoverers (and it is worth protecting them from such a fate), and secondly – are considered to be the most distinctive element of the Andean technocomplexes. However, it is worth recalling here the statement of Neira Avendao, that very often, projectile points (*puntas de proyectil*) make up as much as 45–50% of the general number of tools in surveyed sites of the *puna* zone (Neira Avendaño 1998). As one can see, the combinations presented fit this observation exactly, thus perhaps the treatment of the sample gathered as being, to some extent, representative of the studied terrain is not completely unfounded. The part of the Appendices in which non-obsidian materials used by man in the Valley are presented completes the picture of the raw stone materials in the Valley of the Volcanoes.

The terrain points where obsidian was encountered can be divided into three groups:
A. Those in which tools, flakes and natural fragments were found (O.1-O.4, O.11, O.12, 4/05, 5/05, D01, P1, P2-3, P4, P5, P6, P7, P10, P11, P12, P14, W3, W4, W5, W6-7, W8, W11-12, W15=V9, V2, V3, V4, V8)
B. Those in which only flakes and possibly natural fragments were found (1, 6-7, 8, N-SG/D, O.5-O.6, O.9, O.10, 1/05, W2, W9, W14, P13, U1)
C. Those in which only natural fragments were found (2, 3-4, O.7, O.8 (?), 2/05, 3/05, W1, W10, W13, P.15, V1, V5-6, V7)

The points defined above as group A are usually localized on different types of level areas raised somewhat above the surrounding territory in the form of promontories, hills or small crests. They are less commonly situated on the terraces of streams, in shallow ravines of the *puna* zone. In two cases, type A points have been confirmed near outcrops of raw obsidian sources (W11-12 – Quebrada Ushpa Corral and V4 – Sonco Palca). Most often, locations of this type are good or very good observation points (Figs 7, 10, 75, 76). Moreover they are usually located close to sources of moving water (at one time perhaps also standing water – lakes). The large number of artifacts visible on the surface[37] inclines one to define these places as archaeological surface sites.

Type B points are predominately individual, chance findings. They were made on trails and on valley slopes. In one case, flakes were found directly by an outcrop of obsidian (W2 – Cerro Sayacata), and in another case – by an outcrop of chalcedony vein (O.9 – Huancarama). It should also be noted that point 1/05, located in the immediate vicinity of the Sarpane municipality, is most likely an archaeological site from which most of the artifacts visible on the surface have been removed. Individual, shaped rocks were encountered at the known archaeological sites of Tauca (3-4), Antaymarca (6-7) and Jello Jello (8).

Points grouped under type C are usually outcrops of obsidian- or chalcedony-bearing rocks. They are located on valley slopes or in the more prominent elevations on the pampa, more rarely, however, in the area of ridges and crests. They are sporadically accompanied by flakes (3/05 – Utco, O.8 – Huancarama, W1 – Cerro Huancahuire).

Fig. 75. Archaeological sites (points P5 and P4 are found more or less in blank spots) in the intermountain valley below the Poracota mine (phot. M. Wasilewski)

Fig. 76. Archaeological site (point O11) on the promontory between the Chalhua Puqaio and Cochasique rivers, with excellent visibility of the extensive and well-irrigated intermountain valley (phot. A. Kukuła-Góral)

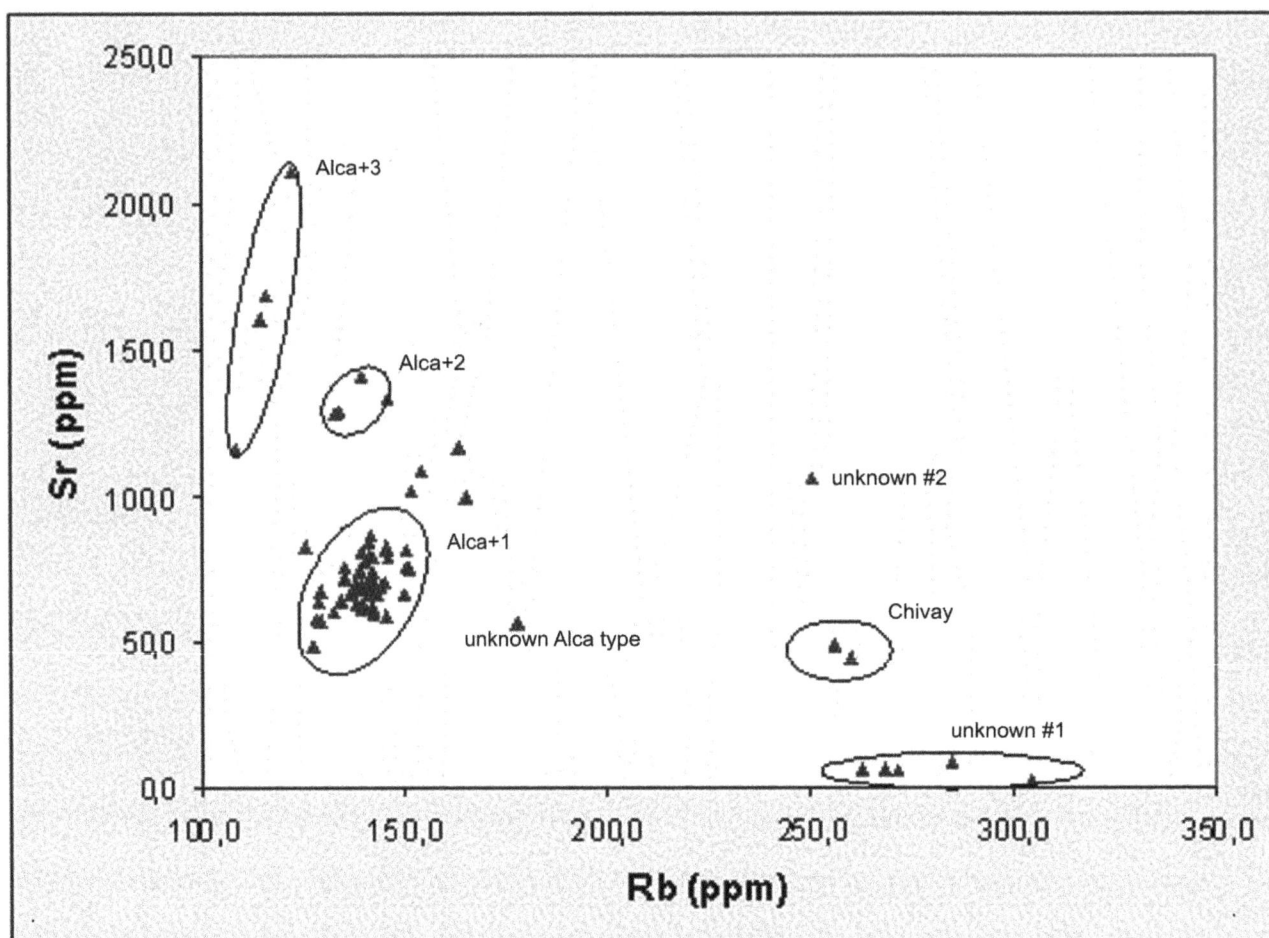

Fig. 77. The results of XRF analysis. The proportion of rubidium content to strontium in particular samples of obsidians from the Valley of the Volcanoes, indicating their relation to the known types of the Alca and Chivay deposits (the values are given in parts per million, ppm)

2.3. Results of tests with the XRF method (X-ray Fluorescence) and NAA (Neutron Activation Analysis)

Presented below are the complete results of the instrumental tests, thanks to which it is now possible to identify in the surest possible way the original sources of particular samples of obsidian, and also to compare them with known places of extraction and occurrence. From the total number of 75 samples sent for testing, 2/3 (50 pieces) turned out to be possible to identify already with the help of the XRF method (Fig. 77). They originated mainly in the Alca and Chivay deposits (including 13 control samples which have not been included in the tables below; see footnote number 19). In relation to the remaining 25 obsidians, it was necessary to conduct NAA analysis due to the ambiguous results of XRF or even their complete uselessness. This was mainly due to the fact that completely new, as-of-yet unrecorded outcrops of obsidians were found on the terrain of the Valley of the Volcanoes (Figs 77–79).

This study depends on the division of the extensive Alca deposits, in Cotahuasi Valley, into several types characterized by a different chemical composition. This classification was developed by researchers several years ago as a result of detailed field and laboratory studies (see, for exam-

ple, Jennings & Glascock 2002). It follows, from the above publication and also from the author's field observations, that Alca-type obsidians appear in more than a dozen points, remote from one another, creating discontinuous layers of nodules (of dimensions up to more than a dozen cm) and colluvia containing fragments up to 6–8 cm in size, seldom larger. Among them are distinguished the types Alca 1 (the most common, connected with the richest deposits), Alca 2 and Alca 3[38].

In the course of analyses commissioned, it turned out to be necessary to create several new taxa. Namely, it has been suggested that Groups 1–6 be differentiated. Among them, Groups 2, 3 and 4 are close in chemical composition to the known Alca types and according to the opinion of Michael D. Glascock they should be treated as the next, new subtypes connected with this deposit area[39]. Groups 1, 5 and 6, however, are completely new, never-before-observed types.

Instrumental chemical analysis by XRF and NAA proves that the decided majority of 62 obsidian artifacts and natural fragments[40] come from the Alca deposit (Fig. 80), mainly the source Alca 1 (Table 3). This is 46 samples, or 74.19% of the total number. All the fragments collected in 2004 (points N–S[41], O.1-4) belong to this type, and thus those found in the middle and lower part of the valley. Also

M. Wasilewski

Table 1

Results of XRF analysis done in the MURR Laboratory (Missouri University Research Reactor)
All values have been given in ppm (parts per million)

Nr MURR	Symbol	K	Ti	Mn	Fe	Zn	Ga	Rb	Sr	Y	Zr	Nb	Pb
WAS001	2	9348.4	18905.1	734.0	17775.5	240.5	0.0	539.0	7253.7	0.0	4243.5	14.0	117.7
WAS002	1/05-a	36459.9	772.6	421.3	5441.9	46.8	15.8	136.5	67.7	14.3	100.6	14.4	18.0
WAS003	1/05-b	37603.9	770.3	466.7	5417.7	44.1	16.7	138.8	68.0	17.1	95.8	14.2	14.5
WAS004	4/05-a	41770.2	855.9	506.4	6038.4	35.1	20.2	150.5	81.3	18.4	131.4	16.0	6.0
WAS005	4/05-b	36734.2	791.8	462.8	5586.4	48.0	16.0	143.8	68.9	18.2	105.5	16.0	17.0
WAS006	5/05-a	38556.1	820.1	482.8	5788.8	45.6	17.4	141.7	73.3	16.0	113.1	15.7	14.8
WAS007	5/05-b	35061.5	761.3	430.6	5393.4	48.9	14.7	137.6	70.1	16.6	92.2	14.2	22.5
WAS021	D.01-a	34298.7	752.2	428.2	5327.8	53.2	13.6	125.4	82.1	14.6	78.7	14.4	19.7
WAS022	D.01-b	34735.1	689.9	446.5	4928.1	44.5	14.9	128.8	56.7	14.4	88.6	13.8	21.5
WAS023	N-S-a	33702.6	833.1	532.5	5581.4	47.6	14.0	115.8	168.1	10.4	102.0	11.0	17.2
WAS024	N-S-b	49354.7	770.8	408.3	5484.4	0.0	28.6	146.0	78.5	17.0	144.1	15.7	0.0
WAS025	N-S-c	50953.5	792.4	447.0	5620.9	0.0	31.1	150.5	75.1	17.6	164.9	14.9	0.0
WAS026	0.11-a	33814.0	781.2	447.4	5513.6	54.2	13.6	139.4	61.9	16.1	92.6	14.6	26.7
WAS027	0.11-b	35158.8	729.3	456.7	5124.0	45.7	14.9	139.2	61.8	14.9	90.3	12.5	23.2
WAS028	0.11-c	32628.5	770.8	428.7	5466.7	57.6	12.5	132.3	60.0	15.8	85.3	14.6	32.0
WAS029	0.11-d	36885.4	765.2	463.7	5375.3	47.5	16.3	139.3	61.5	14.6	99.5	14.9	16.8
WAS030	0.11-e	37429.2	847.7	456.4	5795.9	46.3	16.8	139.2	140.4	16.8	117.3	14.2	12.4
WAS031	0.12-a	35929.9	630.4	491.1	5353.8	48.5	13.8	129.1	67.4	18.8	93.1	18.8	21.1
WAS032	0.12-b	32958.8	832.1	462.6	5927.3	40.3	11.3	138.3	68.9	14.2	86.1	9.5	7.8
WAS033	0.12-c	30242.0	797.9	424.8	5602.6	38.8	10.9	133.8	64.1	12.1	73.9	6.8	4.7
WAS034	0.12-d	33422.7	752.5	464.8	5529.5	44.2	15.3	134.9	75.5	13.3	99.7	8.9	8.0
WAS035	0.12-e	33388.9	766.6	448.6	5521.6	40.4	15.2	139.0	80.4	18.8	90.5	8.2	9.2
WAS036	0.1-4-a	29629.6	1180.9	413.6	7036.0	42.5	5.8	136.9	66.5	18.9	85.1	11.5	0.0
WAS037	0.1-4-b	34070.1	981.1	412.4	6704.4	46.3	8.4	142.0	66.2	14.2	88.5	16.1	11.3
WAS038	OR	32387.5	714.2	427.1	5187.1	41.4	15.8	141.2	72.1	14.4	91.4	9.7	11.0
WAS039	P1	32505.1	868.8	447.6	6075.9	63.9	11.8	140.4	66.1	15.3	92.6	14.7	30.0
WAS040	P2-3	34925.7	763.2	449.1	5393.7	52.0	14.7	138.9	69.7	15.9	93.8	14.4	23.3
WAS041	P4-a	37592.3	794.4	478.5	5603.1	46.0	16.5	141.9	69.5	16.4	104.0	14.5	15.5
WAS042	P4-b	35987.6	843.3	449.9	5839.1	55.1	15.4	133.7	128.2	15.8	113.6	16.1	16.9
WAS043	P4-c	39817.6	859.8	393.5	6091.9	35.3	19.3	250.6	105.8	25.5	145.9	16.2	27.9
WAS044	P7	33737.6	680.7	419.1	5124.3	47.5	14.8	134.7	75.4	16.7	96.8	14.8	18.1
WAS045	P12-a	38897.3	846.5	431.7	5801.6	39.7	18.0	145.8	132.7	16.8	123.7	14.3	14.4
WAS046	P12-b	35712.2	782.2	434.4	5505.7	49.5	15.0	141.8	61.9	17.5	98.0	13.6	19.3
WAS047	U1-a	38582.8	716.0	428.2	5051.4	37.3	17.7	137.5	62.9	16.2	92.0	14.0	12.0
WAS048	U1-b	32607.3	725.0	451.4	5106.9	37.8	13.0	140.9	70.4	13.4	88.3	6.7	8.8
WAS049	V2-a	33080.7	714.8	474.5	5041.1	55.3	13.3	128.4	63.4	13.9	75.1	14.7	25.9
WAS050	V2-b	33241.0	823.1	456.3	5727.5	60.9	12.8	142.1	59.5	16.2	92.0	14.0	26.6
WAS051	V3	34747.4	795.8	450.7	5437.4	40.6	16.4	140.7	79.2	14.8	93.1	8.5	9.1
WAS052	V4-a	31052.6	1019.6	431.2	5801.5	45.8	13.0	141.8	78.4	16.6	86.4	12.0	3.9
WAS053	V4-b	40130.4	561.5	591.5	5595.9	33.4	20.3	268.3	6.2	32.0	124.3	20.5	28.7
WAS054	V5-a	37561.0	525.3	599.8	5517.7	39.2	18.4	262.7	6.2	30.4	113.3	20.9	26.2
WAS055	V5-b	39426.2	539.5	543.5	5527.2	31.4	19.6	285.0	8.8	30.2	103.2	19.2	25.4
WAS056	V7-a	40360.9	583.1	539.0	6503.0	34.7	19.0	304.5	2.7	36.2	127.1	20.2	24.9
WAS057	V7-b	38397.5	490.0	609.4	5512.3	35.3	18.9	271.4	5.7	31.4	116.3	19.5	27.3
WAS058	V8-a	35692.4	785.7	485.5	5530.3	42.6	16.7	141.0	83.5	13.1	100.8	9.3	11.2

53

Table 1 continued

Results of XRF analysis done in the MURR Laboratory (Missouri University Research Reactor)
All values have been given in ppm (parts per million)

Nr MURR	Symbol	K	Ti	Mn	Fe	Zn	Ga	Rb	Sr	Y	Zr	Nb	Pb
WAS059	V8-b	32324.9	862.2	418.5	5753.3	42.5	13.8	145.4	81.9	13.0	89.0	9.2	9.6
WAS060	W1-a	35128.5	800.3	466.2	5546.6	52.0	15.0	132.6	128.0	15.9	102.5	14.8	18.9
WAS061	W1-b	38382.6	804.1	487.7	5505.3	33.5	17.0	163.3	116.7	15.9	101.4	11.5	18.5
WAS062	W2-a	44711.3	665.7	474.4	4670.3	17.4	22.7	178.0	56.5	18.2	72.3	10.2	9.8
WAS063	W2-b	40510.6	669.4	497.3	4054.0	36.2	22.9	165.3	99.3	12.9	72.5	9.8	20.8
WAS064	W2-c	35450.8	757.7	429.2	5227.5	38.3	18.1	141.2	86.2	10.1	90.4	7.2	11.6
WAS065	W2-d	33962.2	854.3	528.2	5965.2	61.5	13.4	150.0	65.8	17.8	101.2	15.1	25.3
WAS066	W2-e	33390.8	758.5	418.8	5302.0	59.0	13.5	139.1	62.4	15.7	88.2	15.3	25.7
WAS067	W5-a	33289.1	818.2	462.8	5752.2	63.5	13.0	138.5	73.9	16.2	92.8	16.0	25.9
WAS068	W5-b	34368.5	721.4	450.2	5120.3	50.7	14.8	136.6	67.3	14.7	88.2	15.6	25.4
WAS069	W6-7-a	36051.1	757.6	473.0	5380.2	47.7	15.5	134.9	71.4	14.5	93.8	13.6	19.4
WAS070	W6-7b	35771.8	741.2	457.5	5230.6	46.9	15.9	141.0	71.2	16.0	93.7	15.2	21.2
WAS071	W10	33791.9	710.8	444.0	5056.1	45.5	14.0	136.9	66.0	14.7	79.9	12.0	28.8
WAS072	W12	35956.8	808.4	470.3	5612.7	37.4	14.8	154.2	108.0	17.6	93.2	11.0	22.3
WAS073	W13	32649.8	758.4	440.3	5247.6	38.1	12.7	151.7	101.2	15.3	75.1	10.0	31.1
WAS074	W14	27574.4	725.7	438.7	5101.7	67.5	9.5	134.7	70.8	14.4	64.4	14.0	44.7
WAS075	W15	36775.7	790.5	470.1	5537.2	48.3	16.0	145.3	59.1	17.3	105.7	15.1	16.7

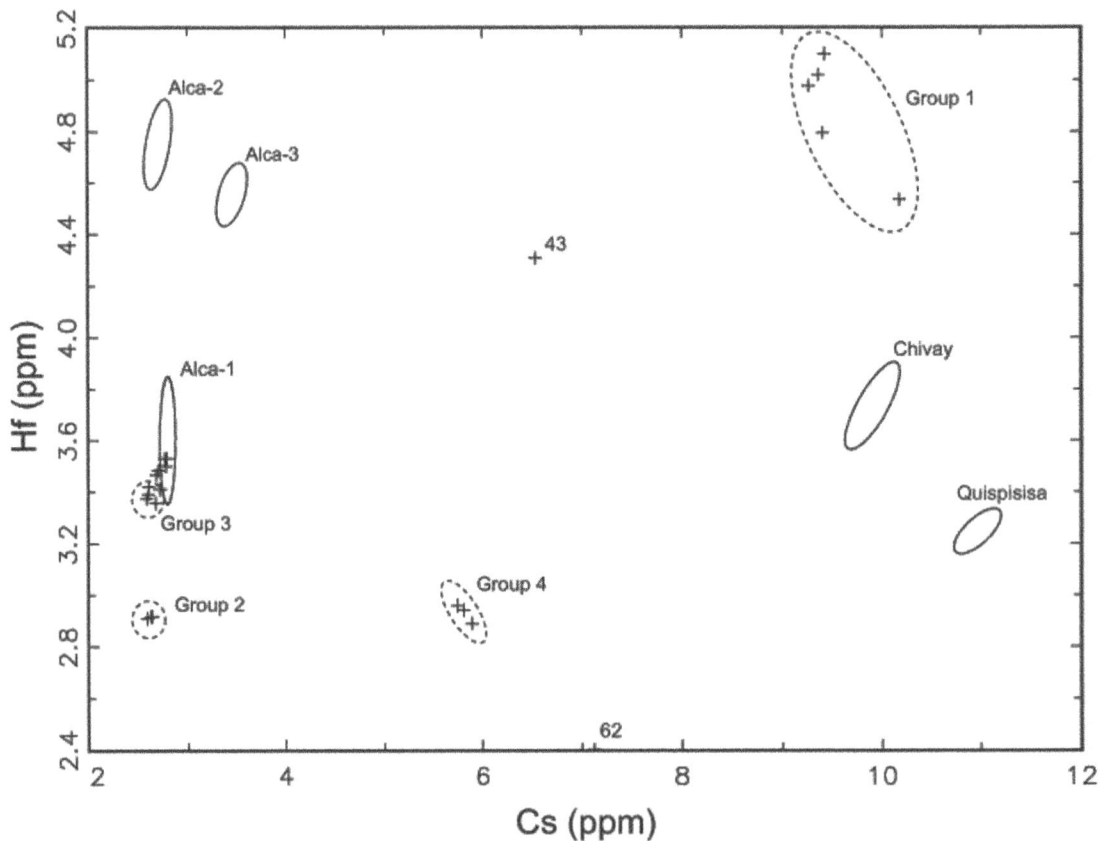

Fig. 78. Results of NAA analysis. The proportion of caesium content to hafnium in particular samples of obsidians from the Valley of the Volcanoes, indicating their typological position in relation to the known types of the Alca and Chivay deposits (the values are given in parts per million, ppm)

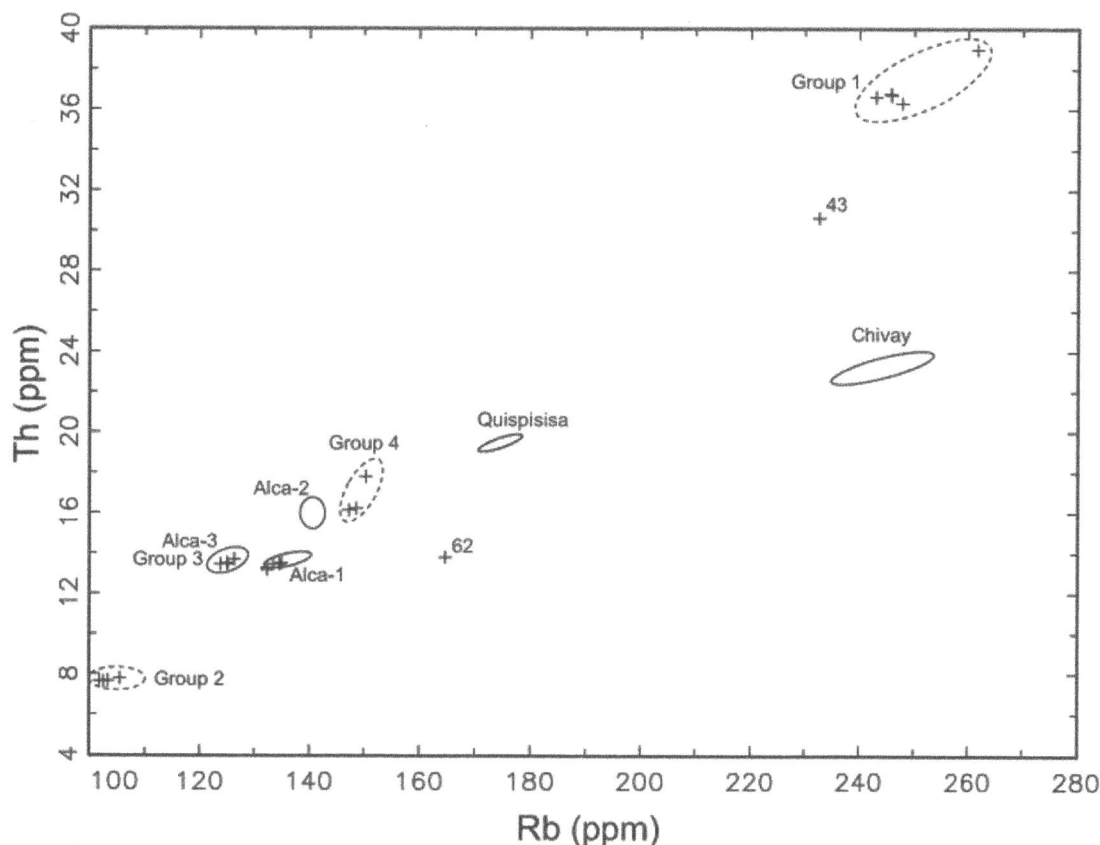

Fig. 79. Results of NAA analysis. The proportion of rubidium content to thorium in particular samples of obsidians from the Valley of the Volcanoes. Chemical dissimilarity of some of the rocks from the already known obsidian deposits is clearly visible (values given in parts per million, ppm)

the site near the Arma village, on the plateau between the volcanoes Nevado Coropuna and Nevado Solimana (point D.01), yielded only such obsidians as well. All of these points on the terrain have been classified as sites, likely sites or loose findings.

Unfortunately, two green fragments (point 2, and the control CH01-c which was not considered in the tables), deceptively similar, macroscopically, to obsidians of such color that appear on other terrains, turned out to be anthropogenic glass, as indicated by the Sr, Zr and Zn content, as well as the small amount of K.

The upper part of the valley (from Lomas Pinculluna and above), brought the most various results. Some of the sites, located on the floor of the main valley and on its slopes, were supplied with raw obsidian originating exclusively from the Alca 1 deposit (points O.12, 1/05, 4/05, 5/05, OR, U1, or, correspondingly, the vicinity of the Panahua village, Sarpane village (2 points), valley slopes above the Sarpane village, the Orcopampa terrain, the vicinity of Cuchurancho). It is worth indicating that there is a complete lack of local outcrops of obsidian on this terrain, although during the field studies outcrops of other silica rocks were encountered (see the Appendices).

The next region, plateaux and flat-bottomed intermountain valleys located in the region of the Poracota mine (points P1, P2-3, P4-a, P7, P12-b; Fig. 81), were supplied with raw material of the type Alac 1, Alca 2 and the related Group 3 (P4-b and P12-a). It is necessary, however, to point

out that on the site marked with the working symbol P4, obsidian of an as-of-yet unknown chemical composition was also confirmed (sample P4-c=WAS043), and on this basis was distinguished as a new type – Group 5.

The most important, and at the same time most interesting area is the Pampa Jararanca plateau, together with the adjacent, upper segments of valleys (Fig. 82). Both archaeological sites and outcrops and secondary colluvial deposits of obsidian were documented there. The archaeological sites described (points O.11, W5-W7, W14, W15, V2-V3, V4, V8, or, correspondingly the promontory between the Chalhua Puqaio and Cochasique rivers, the source of the river Umachulco, Pampa Jararanca, Cerro Chanchaclla, Quebrada Paco, Sonco Palca, Pabellon) contain mainly raw material of the Alca 1 type (in O.11. there are also Group 3 rocks). However, the testing of materials obtained from the outcrops and colluvias on this terrain bring more interesting results. While it is true that the larger part of findings from points W2 (=WAS063-WAS066, Cerro Sayacata; Fig. 83) and W10 (=WAS071, Mistisa Palca-Cerro Mesani; Figs 84, 85) belong undoubtedly to the Alca 1 type, the outcrop marked with number W1 (=WAS060 and WAS061, Cerro Huancahuire; Fig. 86) can remain, due to its chemical composition, counted among the new Alca subtypes: W1-a – Group 3 and W1-b – Group 4. Also the chemical properties of the pebbles in colluvia W12 and W13 (=WAS072 and WAS073, Quebrada Ushpa Corral; Fig. 87) prove that they are likely to be a new Alca 2 subtype (they were attributed

Table 2

Results of NAA analysis for selected samples of obsidian, done in the MURR Laboratory (Missouri University Research Reactor)
All values have been given in ppm (parts per million)

Nr MURR	Ba	La	Nd	Sm	U	Yb	Ce	Co	Cs	Fe	Hf	Rb	Sc	Sr	Ta	Th	Zn	Zr	Al	Cl	Dy	K	Mn	Na
WAS001	688.8	16.0	13.7	2.94	3.87	1.17	31.2	9.504	0.16	18615.3	5.07	9.0	4.70	2824.0	0.435	3.43	51.6	199.6	28498.6	3270.8	2.27	4926.1	845.0	23117.5
WAS023	1000.7	24.3	15.7	2.76	1.71	1.03	45.6	0.413	2.68	5984.4	3.36	105.5	1.87	173.9	0.659	7.78	36.9	116.9	70499.5	328.4	1.69	35330.7	562.3	31384.3
WAS024	961.5	28.3	18.0	3.45	3.40	1.05	55.5	0.218	2.70	5230.7	3.48	132.3	1.72	74.0	0.912	13.27	40.5	111.7	78711.9	603.5	2.48	38697.9	490.5	32007.9
WAS025	989.4	28.8	19.9	3.50	3.48	1.08	56.6	0.222	2.79	5442.2	3.53	135.0	1.77	80.9	0.942	13.51	40.8	125.8	73837.0	609.1	2.08	37900.3	466.7	30395.7
WAS030	992.7	34.1	21.5	3.64	3.12	1.01	64.7	0.179	2.58	5450.2	3.38	123.8	1.72	138.1	0.883	13.46	45.5	119.9	71960.4	537.5	1.92	37618.1	476.6	31374.1
WAS040	996.5	27.9	19.5	3.44	3.53	1.01	54.7	0.244	2.72	5328.8	3.41	132.4	1.73	78.0	0.908	13.17	40.6	112.2	70092.6	538.7	1.73	35381.4	480.2	31147.3
WAS042	1015.8	34.5	21.5	3.67	3.15	1.04	64.8	0.187	2.60	5485.4	3.39	125.1	1.73	145.9	0.879	13.45	43.6	123.2	74265.2	507.2	2.03	38453.7	484.6	32463.8
WAS043	434.4	44.0	20.5	3.38	8.82	1.52	73.6	0.341	6.53	6103.0	4.31	232.6	2.16	91.2	1.431	30.65	34.7	186.6	68223.3	605.4	1.71	42102.7	447.0	29578.1
WAS045	1005.5	34.7	21.8	3.70	3.18	1.03	65.8	0.204	2.68	5577.5	3.47	126.3	1.75	131.5	0.910	13.69	45.6	114.3	71758.6	360.5	2.05	36902.9	496.4	33322.4
WAS053	44.7	29.9	18.1	3.72	10.76	1.90	57.7	0.078	9.41	5369.3	4.79	247.8	1.53	0.0	1.634	36.32	43.1	184.6	64075.9	857.2	2.96	40021.1	638.0	31154.8
WAS054	58.5	35.4	20.9	4.05	10.62	1.95	67.9	0.090	9.26	5426.7	4.98	243.1	1.81	0.0	1.629	36.64	59.1	193.7	66441.5	835.7	2.82	39939.6	675.7	31209.5
WAS055	62.5	30.2	16.4	3.46	11.72	1.83	56.0	0.094	10.18	5019.5	4.54	261.8	1.24	0.0	1.697	38.98	37.8	182.4	60723.7	844.9	1.90	38475.3	596.0	30505.6
WAS056	36.5	30.7	17.3	3.82	10.89	1.88	59.4	0.114	9.36	5476.8	5.02	245.9	1.58	0.0	1.675	36.74	43.1	188.0	67773.9	761.2	2.26	42436.1	637.8	29347.2
WAS057	70.0	32.8	19.3	4.02	10.79	1.92	63.5	0.102	9.42	5734.7	5.10	245.8	1.59	0.0	1.646	36.82	44.0	195.6	65934.0	724.3	2.42	36062.2	642.6	31592.8
WAS060	1005.6	34.2	22.0	3.67	3.39	1.05	65.0	0.178	2.61	5453.3	3.42	125.0	1.72	143.3	0.899	13.49	41.9	119.6	70802.0	582.0	2.31	37277.2	487.0	32144.9
WAS061	1000.6	29.3	17.4	3.29	4.71	1.37	54.1	0.235	5.74	5058.7	2.96	150.3	2.11	124.9	1.060	17.80	33.9	120.5	72949.9	469.4	1.85	37397.9	524.8	27036.0
WAS062	907.4	17.2	11.5	2.71	5.23	1.40	34.3	0.672	7.12	5320.2	2.40	164.7	2.35	95.5	1.082	13.80	26.3	84.6	65435.8	328.5	2.08	42104.1	543.8	20867.9
WAS071	976.6	28.8	19.0	3.53	3.35	1.04	56.7	0.204	2.78	5374.6	3.50	134.6	1.76	92.5	0.932	13.46	45.3	112.9	67342.3	596.2	1.67	38645.1	476.1	31296.8
WAS072	925.0	24.8	15.1	3.00	4.76	1.40	46.0	0.399	5.81	5424.0	2.94	147.2	2.24	121.2	1.039	16.14	27.1	120.6	67722.8	369.1	2.20	35275.1	520.9	28145.0
WAS073	933.5	24.9	15.6	3.01	4.83	1.43	46.0	0.358	5.89	5434.1	2.89	148.6	2.26	122.4	1.022	16.23	26.6	111.9	68973.7	330.2	2.06	35223.4	511.0	27669.7
WAS074	988.8	28.6	19.0	3.51	3.60	1.09	56.4	0.216	2.76	5345.7	3.53	133.5	1.75	81.57	0.919	13.44	44.0	107.4	70054.3	672.6	2.31	35009.3	479.1	31776.8

Table 3

Comparison of results of XRF and NAA analysis of particular samples, together with information on the place of origin (detailed explanations are included in the text)

Nr MURR	Label	Source or chemical group based on XRF	NAA results and comments	Source or chemical group (final results)	Nr MURR	Label	Source or chemical group based on XRF	NAA results and comments	Source or chemical group (final results)
WAS001	2	man-made glass (high Ti, Sr, Zr)	NAA confirms man-made glass	man-made glass	WAS047	U1-a	Alca-1		Alca-1
WAS002	1/05-a	Alca-1		Alca-1	WAS048	U1-b	Alca-1		Alca-1
WAS003	1/05-b	Alca-1		Alca-1	WAS049	V2-a	Alca-1		Alca-1
WAS004	4/05-a	Alca-1		Alca-1	WAS050	V2-b	Alca-1		Alca-1
WAS005	4/05-b	Alca-1		Alca-1	WAS051	V3	Alca-1		Alca-1
WAS006	5/05-a	Alca-1		Alca-1	WAS052	V4-a	Alca-1		Alca-1
WAS007	5/05-b	Alca-1		Alca-1	WAS053	V4-b	Unknown Group #1	NAA confirms new group	Group 1
WAS021	D.01-a	Alca-1		Alca-1	WAS054	V5-a	Unknown Group #1	NAA confirms new group	Group 1
WAS022	D.01-b	Alca-1		Alca-1	WAS055	V5-b	Unknown Group #1	NAA confirms new group	Group 1
WAS023	N-S-a	possible Alca-3	NAA disagrees with Alca-3; but still may be related to Alca	Group 2	WAS056	V7-a	Unknown Group #1	NAA confirms new group	Group 1
WAS024	N-S-b	possible Alca-1	NAA confirms Alca-1	Alca-1	WAS057	V7-b	Unknown Group #1	NAA confirms new group	Group 1
WAS025	N-S-c	possible Alca-1	NAA confirms Alca-1	Alca-1	WAS058	V8-a	Alca-1		Alca-1
WAS026	0.11-a	Alca-1		Alca-1	WAS059	V8-b	Alca-1		Alca-1
WAS027	0.11-b	Alca-1		Alca-1	WAS060	W1-a	possible Alca-2	NAA disagrees with Alca-2; but still may be related to Alca	Group 3
WAS028	0.11-c	Alca-1		Alca-1					
WAS029	0.11-d	Alca-1		Alca-1	WAS061	W1-b	possible Alca-2	NAA disagrees with Alca-2; but still may be related to Alca	Group 4
WAS030	0.11-e	possible Alca-2	NAA disagrees with Alca-2; but still may be related to Alca	Group 3					
WAS031	0.12-a	Alca-1		Alca-1	WAS062	W2-a	outlier; new unknown group	NAA confirms new type	Group 6
WAS032	0.12-b	Alca-1		Alca-1	WAS063	W2-b	Alca-1		Alca-1
WAS033	0.12-c	Alca-1		Alca-1	WAS064	W2-c	Alca-1		Alca-1
WAS034	0.12-d	Alca-1		Alca-1	WAS065	W2-d	Alca-1		Alca-1
WAS035	0.12-e	Alca-1		Alca-1	WAS066	W2-e	Alca-1		Alca-1
WAS036	0.1-4-a	Alca-1		Alca-1	WAS067	W5-a	Alca-1		Alca-1
WAS037	0.1-4-b	Alca-1		Alca-1	WAS068	W5-b	Alca-1		Alca-1
WAS038	OR	Alca-1		Alca-1	WAS069	W6-7-a	Alca-1		Alca-1
WAS039	P1	Alca-1		Alca-1	WAS070	W6-7-b	Alca-1		Alca-1
WAS040	P2-3	possible Alca-1	NAA confirms Alca-1	Alca-1	WAS071	W10	possible Alca-1	NAA confirms Alca-1	Alca-1
WAS041	P4-a	Alca-1		Alca-1	WAS072	W12	possible Alca-2	NAA disagrees with Alca-2; but still may be related to Alca	Group 4
WAS042	P4-b	possible Alca-2	NAA disagrees with Alca-2; but still may be related to Alca	Group 3					
WAS043	P4-c	outlier; new unknown group	NAA confirms new type	Group 5	WAS073	W13	possible Alca-2	NAA disagrees with Alca-2; but still may be related to Alca	Group 4
WAS044	P7	Alca-1		Alca-1					
WAS045	P12-a	possible Alca-2	NAA disagrees with Alca-2; but still may be related to Alca	Group 3	WAS074	W14	possible Alca-1	NAA confirms Alca-1	Alca-1
WAS046	P12-b	Alca-1		Alca-1	WAS075	W15	Alca-1		Alca-1

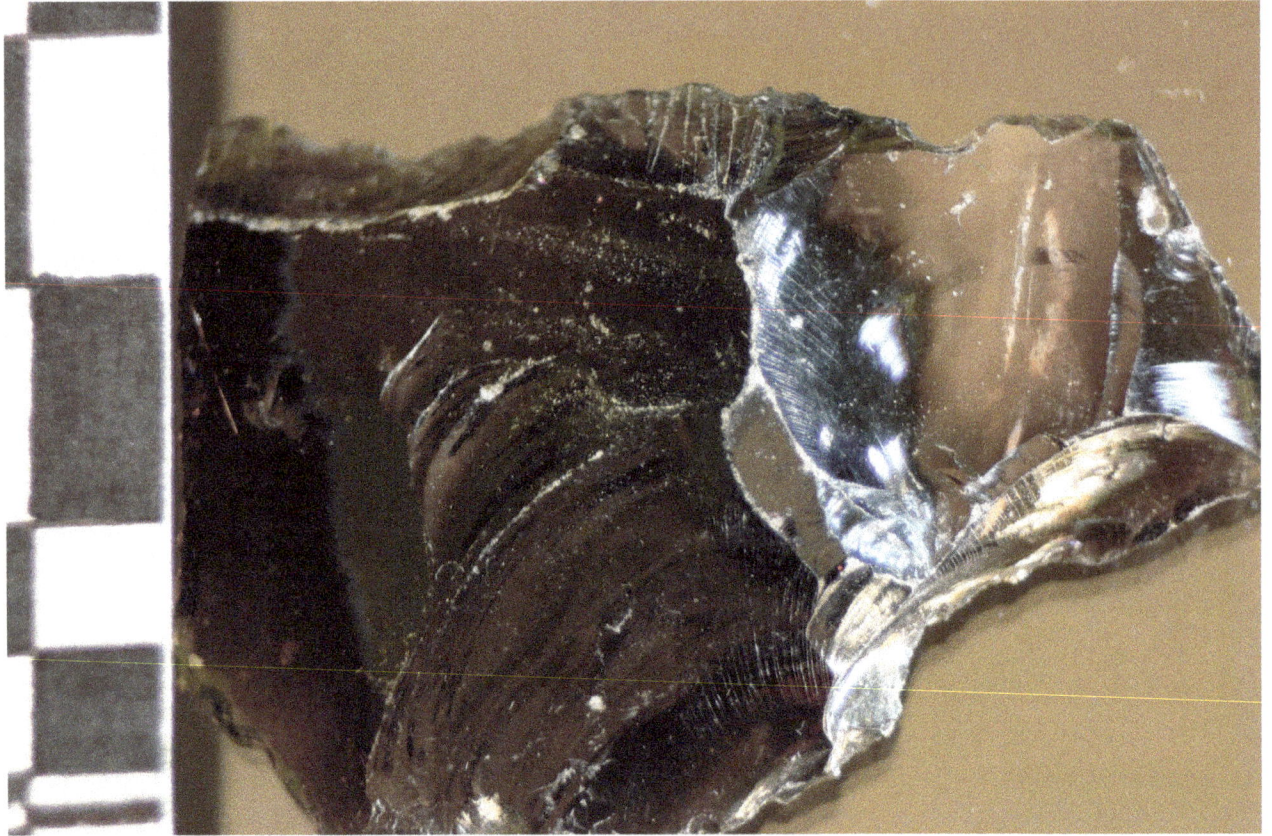

Fig. 80. An obsidian flake found at point W2 belongs to the chemical type of Alca 1 (phot. M. Wasilewski)

Fig. 81. A view of archaeological sites (points P2-3, P4, P5, on the right just outside the photo is P1) in the flat-bottomed intermountain valley in the region of the Poracota mine (phot. M. Wasilewski)

Fig. 82. The plateau of Pampa Jararanca, a view from the north to the south, towards the Valley of the Volcanoes, the eastern slopes of which appear as a mountain chain on the horizon (phot. M. Wasilewski)

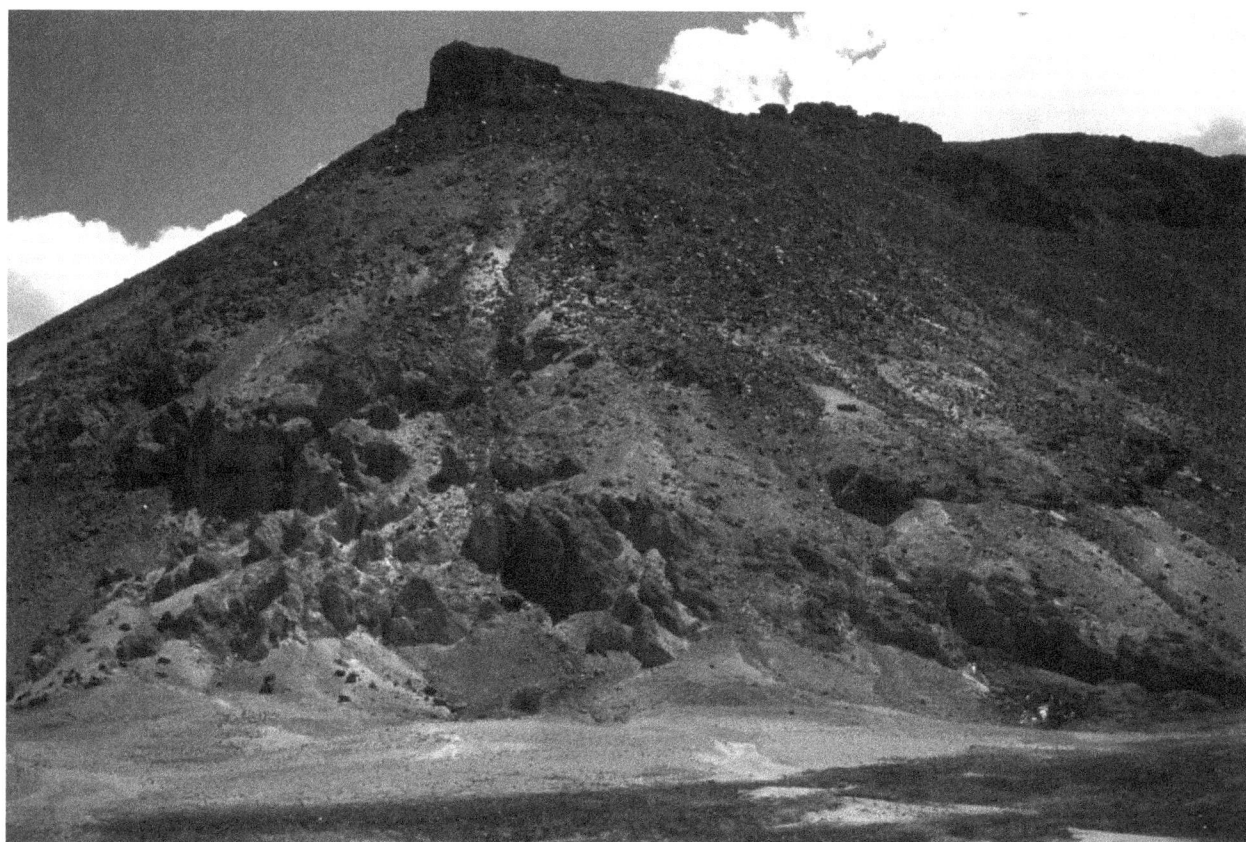

Fig. 83. Cerro Sayacata – the place of localization of obsidian outcrops of the Alca 1 type and the new Group 6. On the grassy space below the hill, something that is likely to be an archaeological site was found (phot. M. Wasilewski)

Fig. 84. The guide, Estani Mario Yucro Yonco-Pollo, holding the largest fragment of obsidian found in the course of the research. In the background are the slopes of Cerro Mesani (phot. M. Wasilewski)

Fig. 85. The largest obsidian block, found at point W10, showing features characteristic of the group Alca 1 (the length of the hammer is 33.4 cm; phot. M. Wasilewski)

Fig. 86. Cerro Huancahuire (outcrop marked as W1), where two new groups of the Alca type were identified: groups 3 and 4 (phot. M. Wasilewski

to the previously-mentioned Group 4). Among the fragments analyzed from point W2 (Cerro Sayacata), moreover, one has been confirmed that is impossible to classify within known groups and types (W2-a = WAS062). A new Group 6 has been proposed for it, which is justified and intriguing insofar as it is an outcrop and colluvia, and thus potential places of obtaining raw material (Fig. 88a, b).

A completely new, as-of-yet unknown type of obsidian was discovered also in the next several points. These are mainly outcrops and colluvia with field numbers V5-6 and V7 (=WAS054-WAS057, Quebrada Huañajahua and Cerro Aljajahua, Fig. 89). The rocks tested were marked as a new, separate Group 1 (Figs 90a–c, 91a–c). Very important in this context is the site bearing the symbol V4 (=WAS053, Sonco Palca), located in the vicinity of these outcrops in which there appear, besides raw material of the Alca 1 type, obsidians belonging precisely to Group 1.

2.4. Typology of stone tools

Taking into consideration the specific, fragmentary character of the archaeological materials collected during the surveys, it was decided that description of debitage would be omitted in this study as irrelevant. It focuses, however, on the illustration, description and interpretation of stone tools. In the collection, as already indicated, projectile points and their fragments predominate. Other types appear decidedly less often or sporadically. The analysis presented here will encompass, for practical reasons, both obsidian

tools and also those from other rock materials (included in the Appendices).

The most information-bearing tools are projectile points, and it is on the basis of their typology that the Pre-ceramic chronology of the Andes is built. They were defined as tools with surface (seldom marginal), flat retouch and with two convergent edges, creating a point. Among 51 projectile points and their fragments, the condition of 39 of them allowed them to be classified into eight types. The rest are damaged in a way that makes their correct identification impossible. It can only be said of them that 7 most likely belonged to the category of large projectile points (length/width/thickness: 3–5 cm/2–2.5 cm/1 cm), 4 – to the medium category (length/width/thickness: 2–3 cm/1.5–2 cm/0.5–1 cm) and 1 – to the small category (length/width/thickness: <2 cm/<1.5 cm/0.3–0.4 cm).

Among the 8 types of projectile points distinguished, the most numerous group (16 pieces) consists of triangular projectile points with a flat or slightly convex base, and straight, slightly convex or sometimes wavy edges, appearing in three sizes – large (length/width/thickness: 3–5 cm/2–2.5 cm/1 cm), medium (length/width/thickness: 2–3 cm/1.5–2 cm/0.5–1 cm) and small (length/width/thickness: <2 cm/<1.5 cm/0.3–0.4 cm) (Fig. 92). Projectile points of this group are characterized by flat bifacial retouch, usually covering the whole surface of the tool, as a rule not very regular. Medium and small examples were made by the technique of pressure flaking. In some examples, a slightly

Fig. 87. Colluvial rocks in Quebrada Ushpa Corral, composed of, among others, obsidian pebbles identified as a new subtype of the Alca 2 deposit (the so-called group 4; phot. M. Wasilewski)

fluted base can be confirmed (4/05, O11, P10(?)). Cross sections of the projectile points are lenticular, sometimes slightly flattened. In this group it is worth pointing out examples from points O11 and possibly W3, with their perpendicularly cut and intentionally retouched points that suggest their use for bird-hunting.

Analogies to projectile points of this group can be indicated in, among others, the works of Aldenderfer (1998, fig. 7.16g; 2000, fig. 5g) and Kaulicke (2000, see. fig. 5/13). The former are connected with the Asana IV Phase/ Muruq'uta Phase and dated to 6650–4900 cal B.C., and the latter with the so-called Capa 6 in Uchkumachay and dated to 6050–5700 cal B.C. It should not be forgotten, however, that projectile points of this type also appear at other Andean sites and are dated much later. A good example is type 8C according to Rick (1980, fig.7.10E–F) originating in the II half of Phase 6, Phase 7 and later periods in the Pachamachay Cave, or dated at the earliest to 1500/1400 cal B.C. These are projectile points with a straight base, triangular in form and supposedly the most characteristic for the whole type 8 group (Rick 1980 p. 162, compare P10, P12, V2, V9,

Fig. 88. Obsidians of the new group 6 from Cerro Sayacata (point W2): a) fragments of obsidians and bedrock; b) obsidian with clearly visible inclusions and unvitrified particles of tuff (phot. M. Wasilewski)

Fig. 89. The first elevation of the Cerro Aljajahua ridge, at its foot on the left there is an archaeological site (point V4) (phot. M. Wasilewski)

W11-12, O11). Similar projectile points with a delicate retouch have been described at the Arcata site by Gerhard Schroeder – Tipo 1, also called Tipo Arcata (*fide* Neira Avendaño 1990, p. 9; *fide* Neira Avendaño 1998, p. 12). This site, and thus also the tools themselves, have been dated approximately to 7050–4900 cal B.C. (or the period defined by the discoverer as Ayampitinense II). The situation looks similar at the La Aguada site (Neira Avendaño 1990). It is also difficult to precisely date these same projectile points from the Guitarrero Cave, the so-called type Quishqui Puncu 15 (Lynch 1980, fig.9.4l). They come from the IV complex (see the discussion below). We find another similarity (particularly to 5/05) in the projectile point of the type Quishiqui Puncu 14/15 according to Lynch (1980, fig. 9.5d). The dating is more certain here, as the artifact comes from the IIe context, or the period of 6200–5600 B.C. (around 7250–6450 cal B.C.). Finally, C. Klink describes very similar projectile points, very widely dated (Final Archaic – Middle Horizon, or 2400 cal B.C. – 1100 cal A.D.) as Group 8 (2007, fig.2.8B). This is the equivalent of type 5B in the earlier collective classification of Klink & Aldenderfer (2005, fig. 3.6D–E), which can be encountered

Fig. 90. Colluvial rocks and tuffs in Quebrada Huañajahua and on the slopes of Cerro Aljajahua containing obsidians of the new group 1 (point V7; phot. M. Wasilewski)

Fig. 91. Examples of obsidians found in the outcrop with working number V7: **a)** obsidian pebbles; **b)** obsidian fragment with clear stratification and fluidal structures; **c)** partly vitrified bedrock, interbedding of volcanic glass and incompletely melted tuff (phot. M. Wasilewski)

at many other sites, such as Hakenasa or Quelcatani. It is acknowledged that projectile points of this type appeared most commonly during the Formative Period (1600 cal B.C. – 500 cal A.D.).

The second most numerous group (15 pieces) is comprised of projectile points with a concave base (the so-called *escotados*) and straight or slightly convex edges (sometimes also called geometric projectile points). They can be internally grouped into three sizes analogous to those mentioned above (Fig. 93). Projectile points of this group were formed by flat bifacial retouch, in nearly all cases covering the en-

tire surface of the tool. The retouch is somewhat more regular than in the first group, and just as in the previous group it was often made with a pressure technique. More often than in the previous group, there is fluting on the base (which is simultaneously responsible for its concave character). In cross sections, projectile points of this group are lenticular, flattened. The W15 projectile points (with serrated edges, creating a "saw") attract attention, as do the P14 (unusually slender), which nevertheless fit within the limits of variation of this type.

The list of analogies, just as in the previous case, is long (Fig. 93). Projectile points with a concave base were described on the Asana site by Aldenderfer (1998, fig. 7.16e and 2000, fig. 5e). These projectile points are connected with the Asana IV/Muruq'uta Phase, and dated to 6650–4900 cal B.C. (or more widely taking into consideration analogies further mentioned – to 8250–3800 cal B.C.). This same author also gives examples of similar projectile points originating in the later phase of Asana VII/Awati Phase, and dated to the period of 3000–1850 cal B.C. (Aldenderfer 1998, fig. 8.25a–d and 2000, fig.7a–d). Such tools commonly appear, after all, in the Lake Titicaca basin. Almost identitical projectile points come from the Arcata and La Aguada sites (Neira Avendaño 1990, p.19; Szykulski 2005). Unfortunately, we do not have any dates from them, and Neira's suggestion of a very early pedigree for this type of projectile point, based on analogies of appearance to Clovis or Lindenmeier projectile points, seem none too convincing. After all, the author himself notes that for now we should refrain from dating them (Neira Avendaño 1990). This same author quotes, after all, other examples of triangular projectile points with a concave base as well[42]. They come from the sites of Sumbay SU-2, where they appeared in the youngest preceramic strata, and Ruinas de Chijra (Departament Arequipa, vicinity of the Coporaque municipality), where they are dated to the Late Horizon (Neira Avendaño 1990, p.164). Often, a noticeable difference is the larger notch of the base than in specimens from the Valley of the Volcanoes. This confirms, however, the opinion of a long time horizon in which projectile points of this type may appear.

Projectile points resembling some examples from point O11 are described by Rick (1980, fig. 7.1C) as type 1A, from phase 1 (Levels 31-33) dated to around 9500–8200 cal B.C. These tools, however, were made mainly from chalcedony and quartz, and in addition, according to the author, this type is unknown outside the area of Puna Junin (Rick 1980, p. 317). At another site of this region (Uchkumachay Cave, Capa 6), there also appeared an artifact very similar to projectile point V8 from the Valley of the Volcanoes (Fig. 93) and dated to 6050–5700 cal B.C. (Kaulicke 2000, fig. 5/17). What is interesting is that it was made of obsidian.

A series of projectile points with a concave base is part of the inventory from the site at Pampa de Lampas and from Guitarrero Cave. They were described as Lampas types 1 and 1b (Lynch 1980, fig. 9.2a–i, 9.6f, 9.7b–c). The difference between the two types lies in the care with which they were made – the less-developed type 1b is considered to be potentially older and it alone appears in the complex IIb. Both types of projectile points appear in Guitarrero in complexes IId, III and IV. The dating of particular cultural strata on the site present serious problems connected with, among other things, natural disturbances of the stratigraphy, the activity of later settlers, *huaceros*, etc. The age of complex IIb is estimated at 8000–7400 B.C. (which corresponds to 8750–8050 cal B.C.), complex IId at 6800–6200 B.C. (which corresponds to around 7900–7200 cal B.C.), the lower limit of age for complex III at 5600 B.C. (which corresponds to 6289–6233 cal B.C.). Unfortunately, the end of the formation of complex III has not been precisely defined. Some of the dates (GX-1451) indicate that it could be situated after the date 4600 B.C., or 5770–5227 cal B.C. Complex IV is the most difficult to interpret, yielding both very early dates (7438–7032 cal B.C.), as well as late ones (770–93 cal B.C.; 529 B.C.–219 cal A.D.) or even contemporary ones (Lynch 1980, Ziółkowski *et al.* 1994, Walanus & Goslar 2004). Most likely, it is very mixed and disturbed, nevertheless Lynch thinks that in the Guitarrero Cave there was likely no settlement after the sixth millennium B.C. (however, robbed graves were also located there, which was one of the reasons for the mixing of sediments).

Many authors describing sites located to the north of our area of study notice a similarity of the projectile points of the *escotados* type that they found to projectile points of the Ichuña type, known from the mountainous areas of southern Peru (Lynch 1980, Rick 1980). They also point out, however, so as not to confuse the two types with each other, that the Ichuña projectile points are dated at the earliest to the Formative Period (1600 B.C. – 500 A.D.), in other words much later than the examples from the north that were mentioned[43].

Undated examples that come from surface findings also appeared at the Ch'uxuqullu site (Island of the Sun, Lake Titicaca). Authors are inclined to include them in the Formative Period (Stanish *et al.* 2002, fig. 5D and F). Finally, a striking analogy is found in the work of C. Klink – the so-called Group 7 (2007, fig. 2.8A). Dating of this form is unusually broad (Burger *et al.* 2000, Klink 2007), encompassing the period from Final Archaic (2400 B.C.), up to the Late Horizon (1500 A.D.). They are most common, however, in the Formative Period (1600 B.C. – 500 A.D.). Projectile points of group 7, according to Klink, are the equivalent of type 5D according to Klink & Aldenderfer (2005, fig.3.6J–N). The comparison to projectile points from the Valley of the Volcanoes can be extended to group 5C, which differ from the former only in size (Klink & Aldenderfer 2005, fig. 3.6F–I). The projectile points described here come from such sites as Hakenasa, Quelcatani and Asana.

The remaining six types of projectile points appear in individual examples. Two projectile points with a stem were found (Fig. 94). These are examples with dimensions of 2.5–3 cm/1.5–2 cm/0.8 cm, originating at points 5/05 and P12. The stem is somewhat less than half the length of the projectile point, is clearly differentiated and rounded at the end. Both artifacts were made with a pressure technique, with the help of moderately regular, flat bifacial retouch, which in the case of the first projectile point does not cover the whole tool. Cross sections can be described as lenticular, asymmetrical.

These projectile points, too, find their equivalents in the works of Aldenderfer (1998, fig. 8.3b and 2000, fig. 6b). Particularly visible in this case is the analogy to the artifact 5/05 (Fig. 94). Such projectile points are connected with the phase Asana VI/Qhuna Phase and dated to 3800–3000 cal B.C. Almost identical examples are described by C. Klink as Group 4 and 6 (2007, fig. 2.7F–G and K). These projectile points are dated to the Late and Final Archaic, or more precisely, 4600–3400 B.P. (or around 3350–1700 cal B.C.) and they are the equivalents of type 4F according to Klink & Aldenderfer (2005, fig.3.5N) from the Asana and Hakenasa sites. Here one might also mention similar projectile points from the nearby site of Arcata, the so-called Tipo 2 according to Schroeder (*fide* Neira Avendaño 1990, p.9). They have, however, a clearly shorter stem with respect to the projectile point, but just like the ones analyzed, they are made of obsidian. Their dating is rather broad and only approximate – 7050–4900 cal B.C. (at the Arcata site, no ^{14}C dates were obtained).

The second projectile point with a stem (P12, Fig. 94), somewhat different than the first, should be compared to the projectile points that were often made of exotic materials from the phase Asana VI/Qhuna Phase, dated to 5850–3000 cal B.C. (Aldenderfer 1998, fig. 8.3c–d and 2000, fig. 6c–d). It is also similar to one of the tools from the Uchkumachay Cave from Capa 5 (Kaulicke 2000, fig.4/13), which, in turn, is dated to the period 5700–3800 cal B.C., and also to the 7A type projectile point according to Rick (1980, fig.7.9C–D), dated to Phase 5 (around 2850–1850 cal B.C.) and 6-7 (around 1850–400 cal B.C.). And finally, we find an analogy in the inventory from the Telarmachay Cave. This is the so-called type BI.7 according to Lavallée (1985, fig.34o), from the IV stratum dated to around 3150–1850 cal B.C. Klink & Aldenderfer classify such projectile points as type 4D (2005, fig.3.5G) and also invoke, as an analogy, type P5 (*Punta Cueva*) from the Toquepala site (Ravines *fide* Klink & Aldenderfer 2005). Here, also similar is the type Sumbay 12 (Neira Avendaño *fide* Szykulski 2005).

At points O1-O4 and O12, pentagonal projectile points were found, with example O1-O4 being almost oval (Fig. 94). These projectile points are small (with a length of 2.5 and 2 cm, a width of 1.5 and 1 cm, and thickness of 0.5 cm for both), formed with flat, irregular bifacial retouch, by a pressure technique. Cross sections are lenticular, and the edges are straight or slightly wavy.

It is possible to find a similarity between O.1-O.4 and O.12 (Fig. 94) and projectile points from the Uchkumachay site (Kaulicke 2000, fig. 4/4 and 14), dated to the period 5700–3800 cal B.C. Projectile points of similar shapes and age (phase 2: 8250–5850 cal B.C. and the beginning of phase 3: 5850–3800 cal B.C.) appear also in Junin, in the Pachamachay Cave (Rick 1980, fig. 7.4E), where they are described as type 3B. Projectile points of type 8B are also very similar (Rick 1980, fig. 7.10C–D), broadly dated to the phases 5-7 (2800–400 cal B.C.), but predominantly to the middle of phase 5 (around 2200 cal B.C.). The next analogy is the type BI.1c projectile points according to Lavallée (1985, fig. 30a, i, o). These tools originate in strata VI and V, and are dated to the period 6050–4000 cal B.C. We can find yet another typological connection in the inventories from Pampa de Lampas and Guitarrero Cave. These are the so-called Lampas 12 projectile points (Lynch 1980, fig. 9.3h–i, 9.6g–h, 9.7f). They were found in Guitarrero in complexes IIb and IIe, which allows them to be dated to 8000–7400 B.C. (which corresponds to 8750–8050 cal B.C.) and 6200–5600 B.C. (around 7250–6450 cal B.C.). Certain stylistic references to type 2B according to Klink & Aldenderfer (2005, fig. 3.3I) can also be seen. Due to the rhomboidal shape, it is recognized by authors as a characteristic feature, however these are not identical tools.

On the basis of a fragment from point P2, it can be assumed that the projectile point found there had been over 2.5 cm in length, with a width of 2.3 cm and a thickness of around 1 cm. It had been made with the help of flat, moderately regular, bifacial retouch, with pressure technique. The projectile point seems to have a thick, weakly differentiated stem, which is additionally slightly fluted at the bottom. The cross section of the tool is lenticular. It can also be counted among the broader group of pentagonal projectile points.

It is not completely certain whether the P2 projectile point (Fig. 94) can be compared to the BI.3 type according to Lavallée (1985, fig. 31g). If this turned out to be justifiable, then the dating of the one appearing in the stratum of the VII type should be taken into consideration: 12 100–6050 cal B.C. In this case, however, caution should be exercised due to the lack of the hafts (barbelures) characteristic for the above-mentioned type at the shoulder in the widest part of the projectile point A similar difficulty arises in attempts to compare projectile points from the Brorota site to the P2 example. One might mention, however, that because the Brorota projectile points were made mainly of obsidian, they have similar size and retouch (Szykulski 2005, fig. 16C). The projectile points described also find an analogy in the inventory of the Sumbay SU-3 site. Similar artifacts there were classified as the type Sumbay II-D (Neira Avendaño 1990, p.37) and are dated approximately to the period 6150–4100 cal B.C. (see also the discussion below).

Another potential similarity is found in the work of Lynch (1980, fig. 9.2j, 9.6i, 9.7e). The projectile points referred to here come from the IIc and IIe complexes, and are dated to around 7400–6800 B.C. (around 8600–7850 cal B.C.) and 6200–5600 B.C. (around 7250–6450 cal B.C.). Another analogy, to the type Quishqui Puncu 14 according to Lynch (1980, fig. 9.4g), is also possible. These tools were found in the Guitarrero IIb complex (8000–7400 B.C. = 8750–8050 cal B.C.). The so-called Group 2 projectile points according to Klink (2007, fig. 2.7B) are another, perhaps more likely, reference. The difference that draws attention in this case, emphasized by the author, is the careless production of the projectile points, which rather cannot be said of the specimen from the Valley of the Volcanoes. Artifacts of this type are dated to the Late Archaic, or around 4400–3000 cal B.C., during which they appear mainly in the period 4600–3350 cal B.C. According to the author, they are to be identified with the type 4D that she described earlier, particularly with examples from the Hakenasa site (Klink & Aldenderfer 2005, fig. 3.5H–I). It is worth pointing out, however, that even these projectile points recognized as large are smaller than the fragment from the Valley of the Volcanoes.

A fragment of a projectile point that can be described as convexo (having a strongly convex, or even sharp, base with straight, convergent edges) was found at point P4 (Fig. 95). It has dimensions of 2.4 cm wide, 0.6 cm thick, and the whole projectile point is at least 3 cm long. This fragment was made with unifacial retouch, moderately steep, marginal, on a flake. The base was slightly fluted. We find potential analogies among type 5A and 5B projectile points according to Rick (1980, fig. 7.8A–F). A fundamental difference lies in the fact that the projectile points referred to are bifacial. This is also the reason for omitting in this comparison other projectile points with a similar form of base (i.e. those described by Lynch 1980). Examples of this type at the Pachamachay site are dated mainly to Phase 4 (3800–2850 cal B.C.), but also to the second half of Phase 3 (4800–3800 cal B.C.) and Phase 5 (2850–1900 cal B.C.). It is possible that just such projectile points were found in Arcata (Schroeder fide Neira Avendaño 1990, so-called Tipo 4), but, unfortunately, there are no sketches of these projectile points for an ultimate comparison (the site itself is dated to the period 7050–4900 cal B.C.). Projectile points from Asana (the so-called type 3D, Klink & Aldenderfer 2005, fig. 3.4H and J) and from Kasapata (the so-called Group 3, Klink 2007, fig. 2.7D) have a similar base, as do those from Ch'uxuqullu (Stanish et al. 2002, fig. 5G). Klink gives important information, writing that projectile points of this type are very uncharacteristic and dated very broadly (Klink 2007, p. 51), by virtue of which they do not have great typochronological value.

A fragment of a tool from point O12 has been classified as a projectile point on the basis of analogy to artifacts from other sites[44]. It was made on a thin flake, with very minimal, marginal retouch, as a rule unilateral, moderately steep; the base is difficult to define (Fig. 95). The artifact has dimensions of 1.5 cm in width, 0.3 cm in thickness, with a preserved length of 1.6 cm. With regards to production technique and the size, this artifact closely resembles the type 8A projectile point according to Rick (1980, fig. 7.10A). They are dated to Phases 5–7 (2850–400 cal B.C.), with indication for the turn of Phases 5/6 (around 1800–1700 cal B.C.). Similar tools come from the Arcata site (Schroeder fide Szykulski 2005), unfortunately there are no absolute dates in this case.

The last type found during the studies is a fragment (half?) of a slender projectile point made of andesite (Fig. 95). This is the largest tool found in the Valley of the Volcanoes during the surface studies carried out within the framework of this research project. The length of the preserved fragment is 4.5 cm, the maximum width is 3.5 cm, and the thickness is around 0.8 cm. The projectile point was formed with flat, not very regular, bifacial retouch that covers the whole surface of the tool. The projectile point is lenticular in cross section. Due to the very characteristic, differentiated (notched) and bifurcated[45] stem, the artifact resembles the stemmed-bifurcate type of North American projectile points (Kirk, St. Albans, LeCroy, Dalton), dated to the Early Archaic (around 8000–7000 cal B.C.; Fiedel 1992, Justice 1995, Hanna 2007). Obviously, nothing more should be

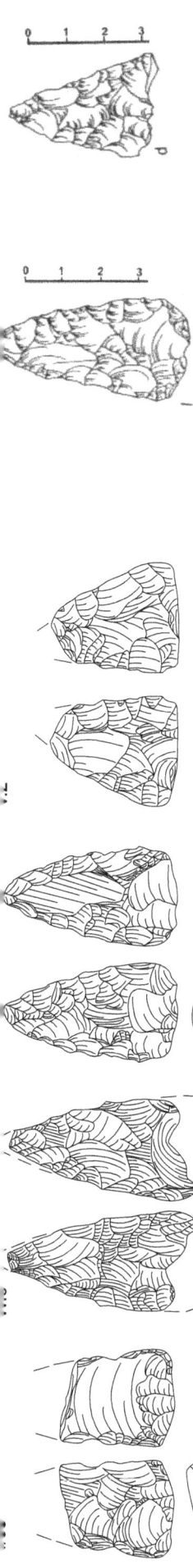

Lynch 1980, fig. 9.5d

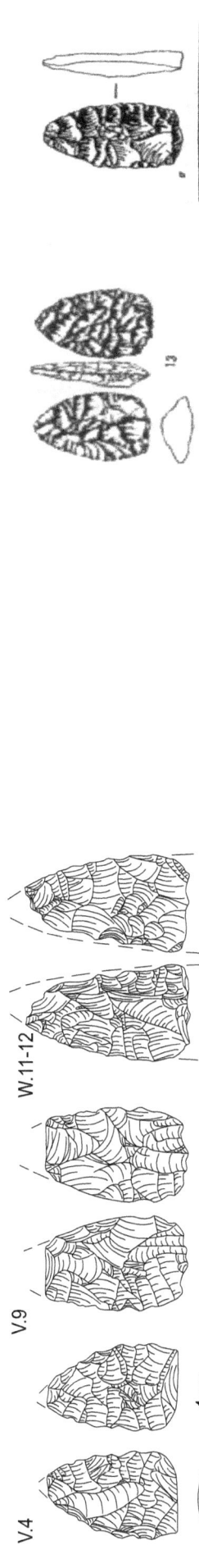

Lynch 1980, fig. 9.4l

Aldenderfer 2000, fig5g

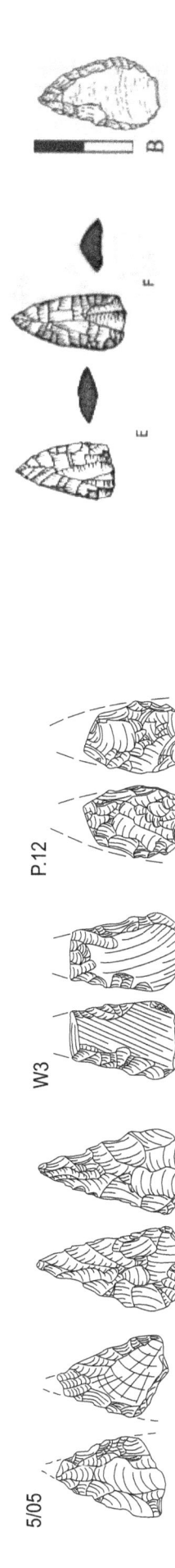

Kaulicke 2000, fig5/13

Klink 2007, fig.2.8B

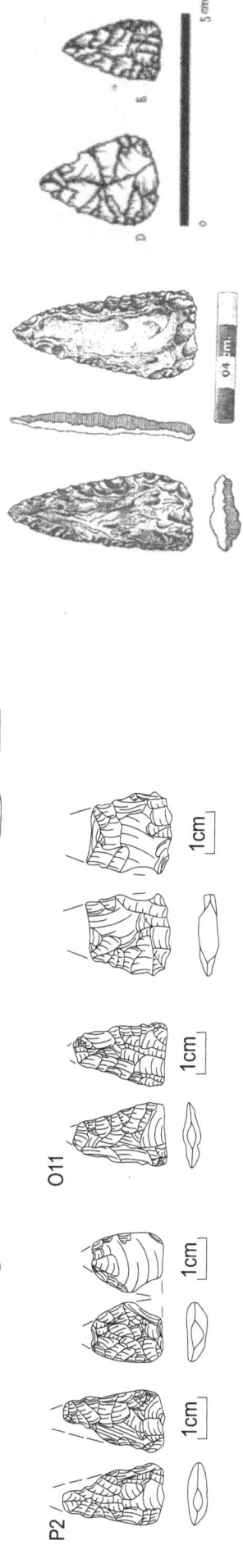

Rick 1980, fig.7.10E-F

Klink & Aldenderfer 2005, fig.3.6D-E

Neira Avendaño 1998, p.12

W.11-12

V.9

V.4

P.12

W3

5/05

O11

P2

O11

Fig. 92. Tools from Valle de los Volcanes – triangular projectile points with a flat or slightly convex base (drawn M. Wasilewski) with analogies from other sites

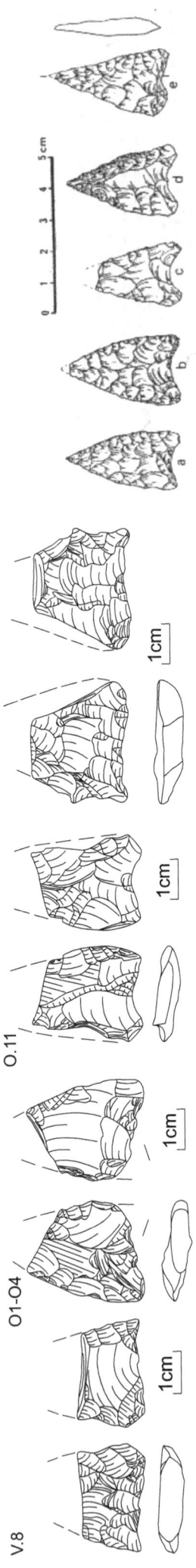

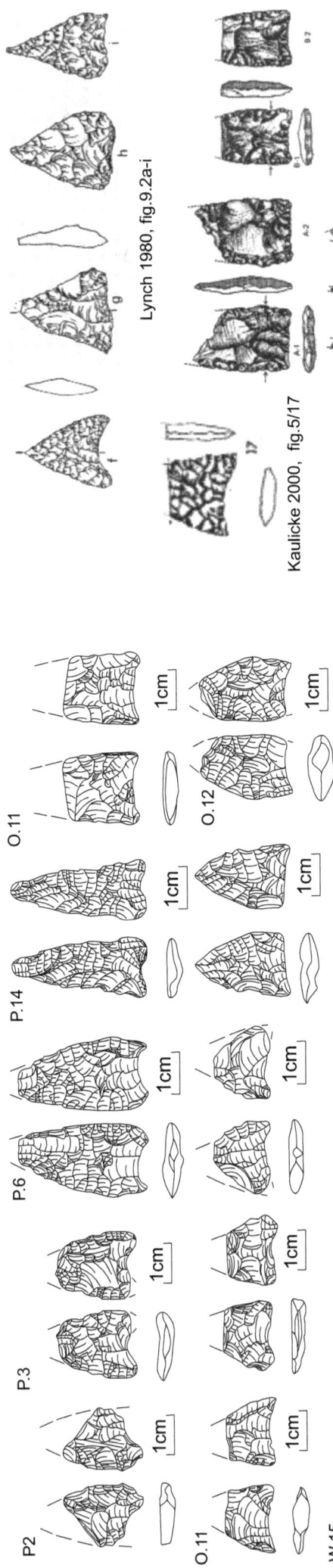

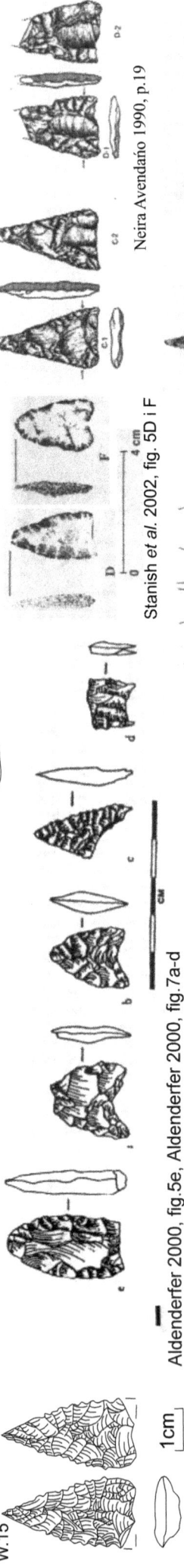

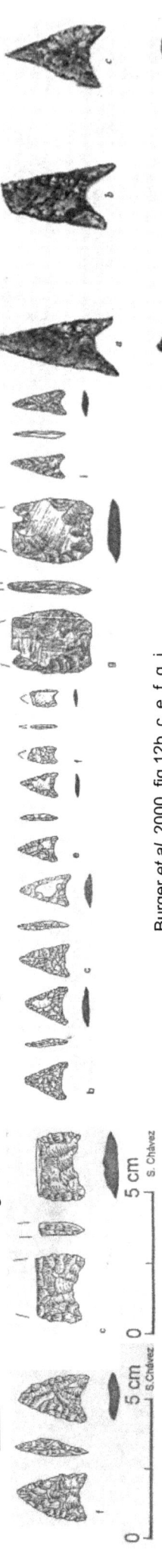

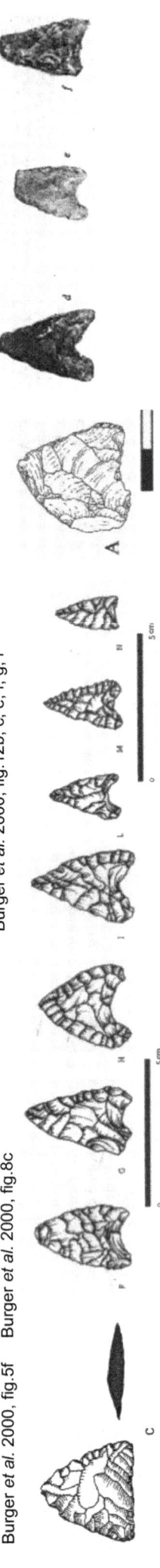

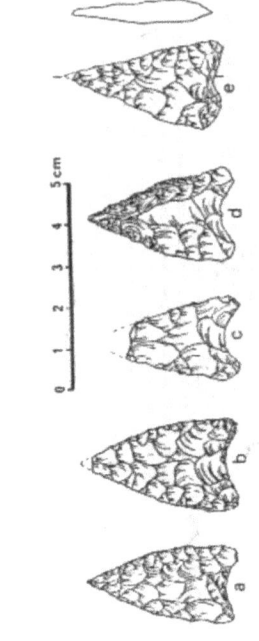

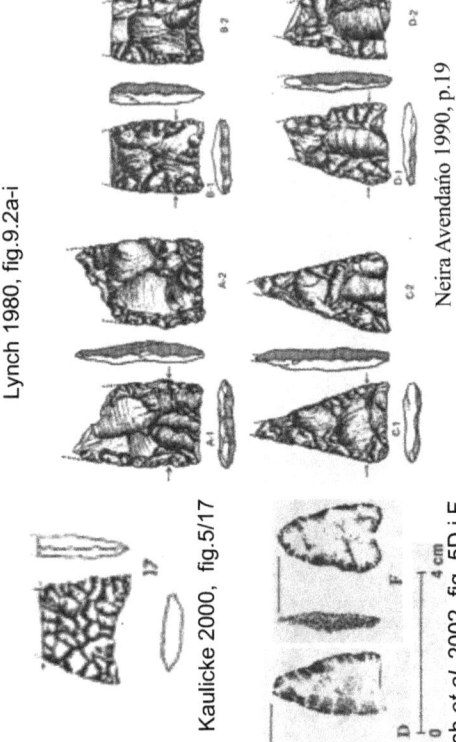

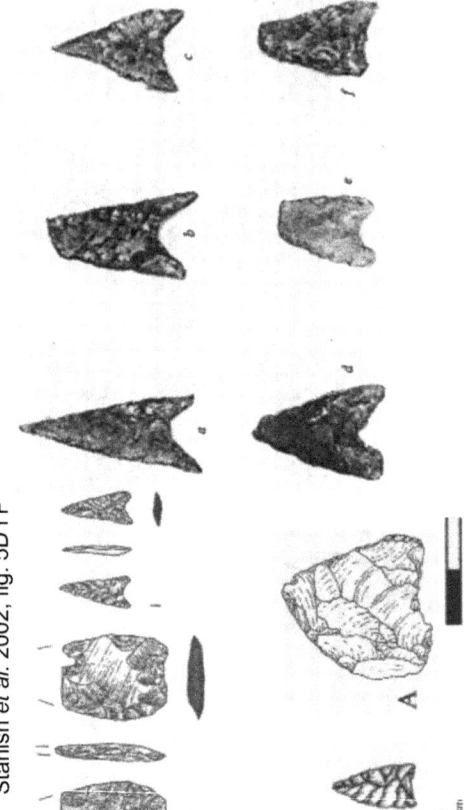

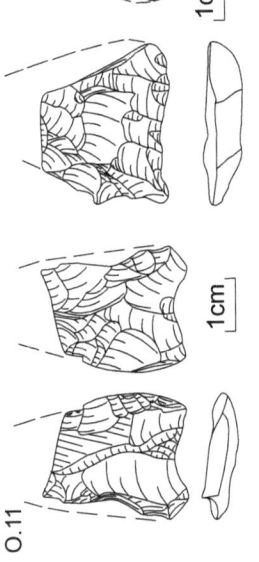

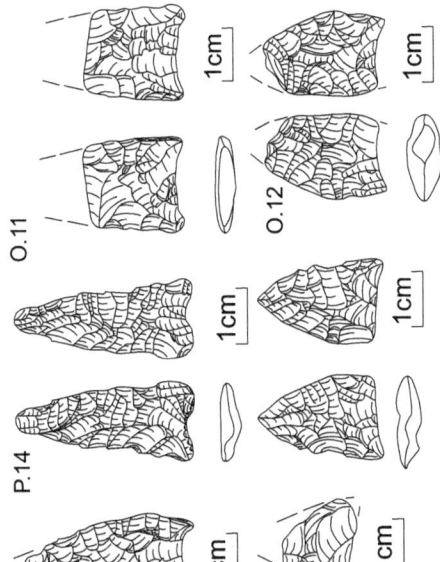

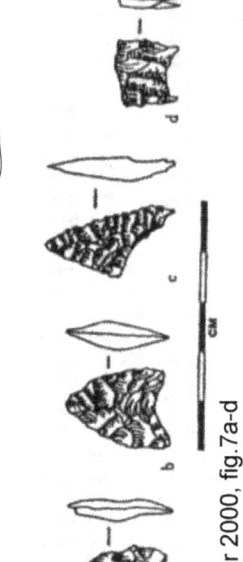

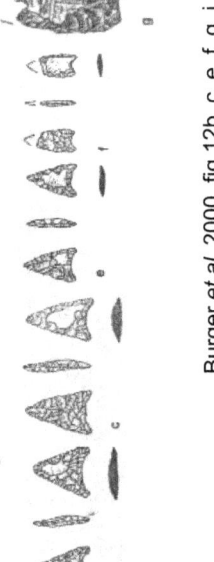

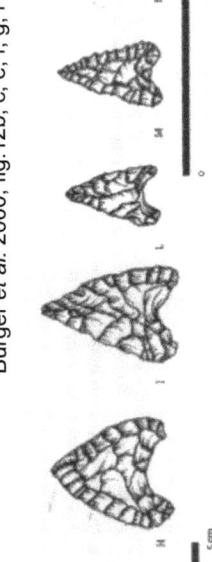

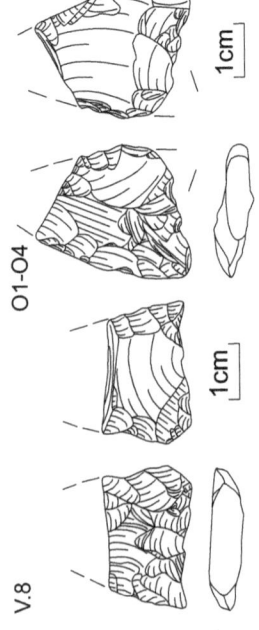

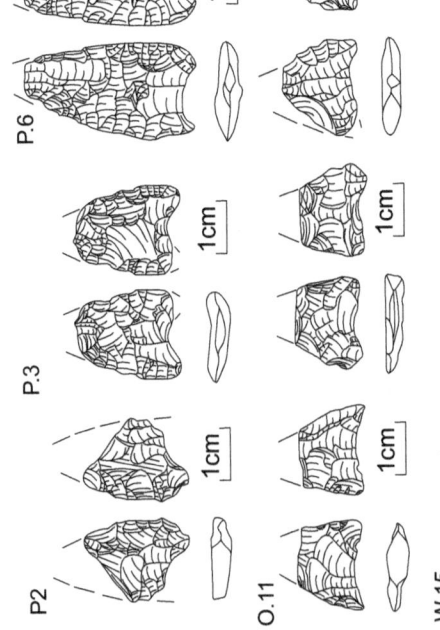

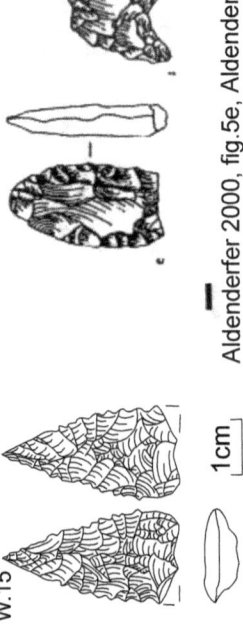

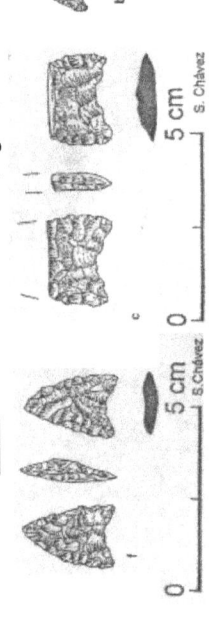

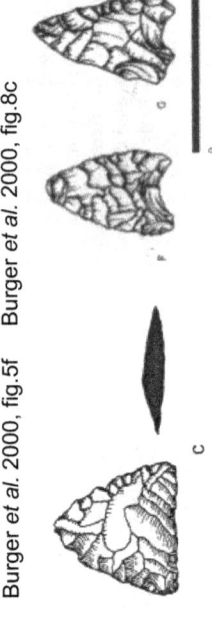

Lynch 1980, fig.9.2a-i

Neira Avendaño 1990, p.19

Kaulicke 2000, fig.5/17

Stanish et al. 2002, fig. 5D i F

Klink 2007, fig.2.8A

O.11

V.8

O1-O4

P2

P.3

O.11

W.15

P.6

P.14

O.11

O.12

Aldenderfer 2000, fig.5e, Aldenderfer 2000, fig.7a-d

Burger et al. 2000, fig.12b, c, e, f, g, i

Burger et al. 2000, fig.8c

Burger et al. 2000, fig.5f

Klink & Aldenderfer 2005, fig.3.6F-G, L-N

Rick 1980, fig.7.1C

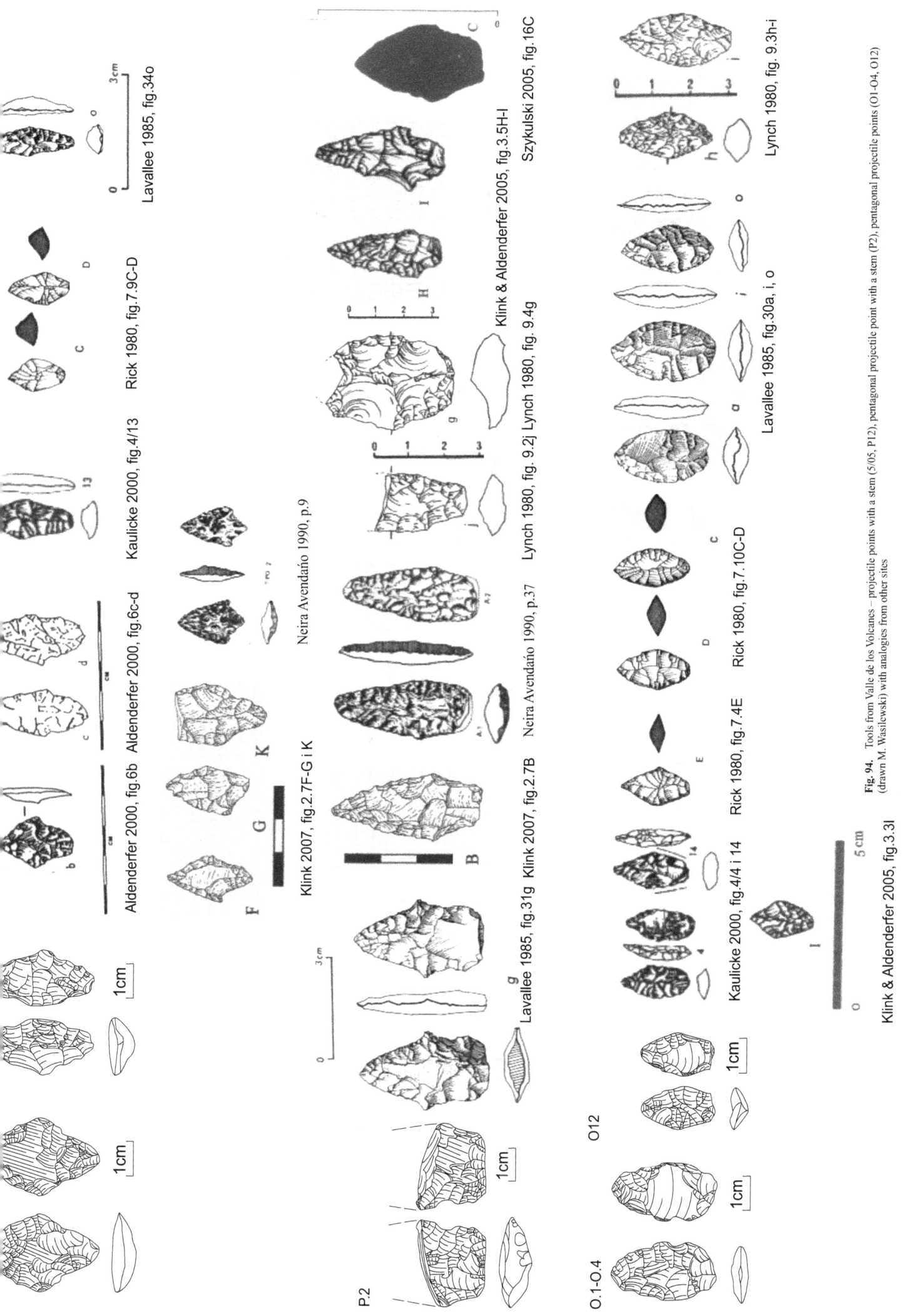

Lavallee 1985, fig.34o

Rick 1980, fig.7.9C-D

Kaulicke 2000, fig.4/13

Aldenderfer 2000, fig.6b Aldenderfer 2000, fig.6c-d

Neira Avendaño 1990, p.9

Klink & Aldenderfer 2005, fig.3.5H-I

Szykulski 2005, fig.16C

Lynch 1980, fig. 9.2j Lynch 1980, fig. 9.4g

Klink 2007, fig.2.7F-G i K

Lynch 1980, fig. 9.3h-i

Neira Avendaño 1990, p.37

Lavallee 1985, fig.31g Klink 2007, fig.2.7B

Lavallee 1985, fig.30a, i, o

Rick 1980, fig.7.10C-D

Kaulicke 2000, fig.4/4 i 14 Rick 1980, fig.7.4E

5 cm

Klink & Aldenderfer 2005, fig.3.3l

Fig. 94. Tools from Valle de los Volcanes – projectile points with a stem (5/05, P12), pentagonal projectile point with a stem (P2), pentagonal projectile points (O1-O4, O12) (drawn M. Wasilewski) with analogies from other sites

Stanish *et al.* 2002, fig.5G

Klink 2007, fig.2.7D

Neira Avendaño 1998, p.19

Hanna 2007, pp.41, 59, 102, 144

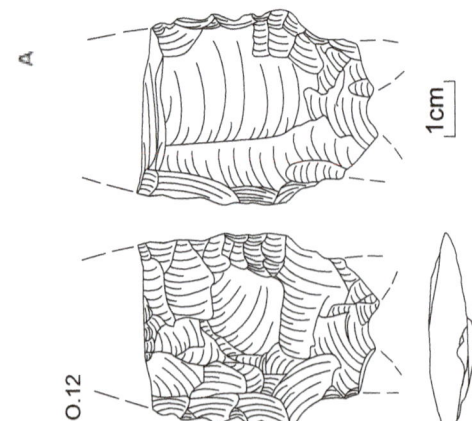

Klink & Aldenderfer 2005, fig.3.4H i J

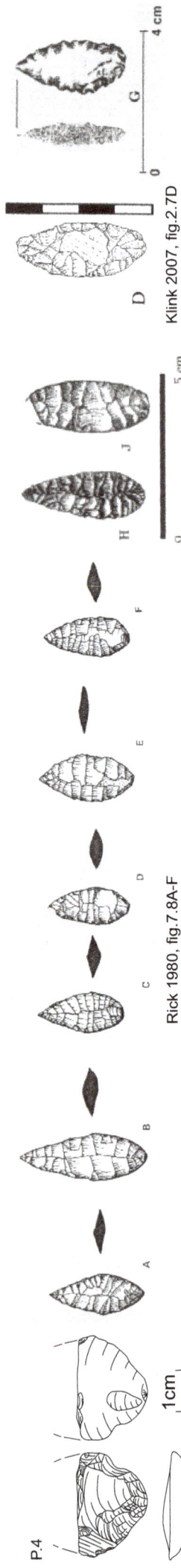

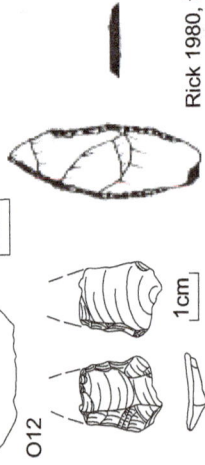

Rick 1980, fig.7.8A-F

Neira Avendaño 1990, p.36

Rick 1980, fig.7.10A

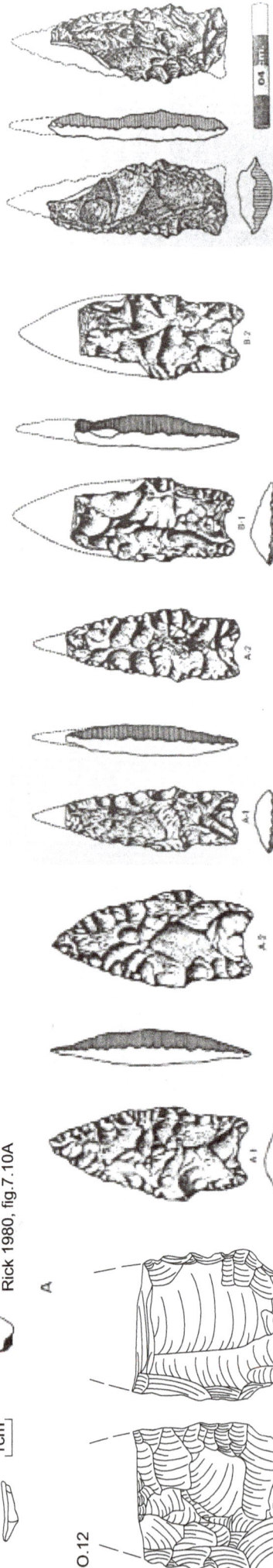

Neira Avendaño 1990, p.35

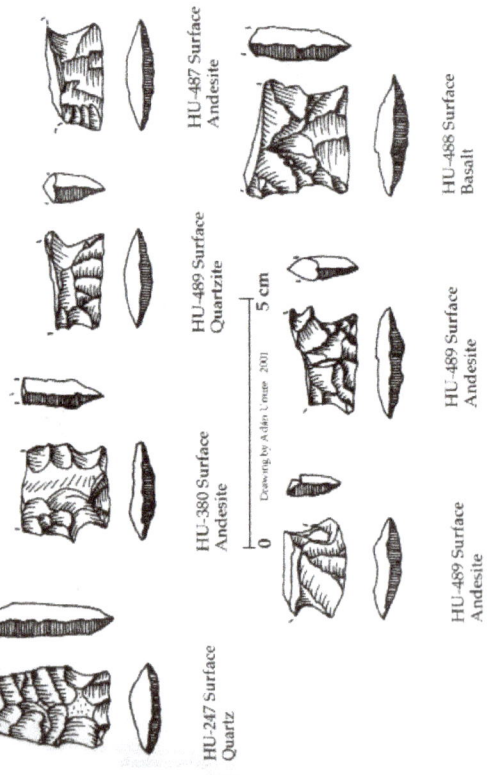

HU-487 Surface
Andesite

HU-488 Surface
Basalt

HU-489 Surface
Quartzite

HU-380 Surface
Andesite

HU-489 Surface
Andesite

HU-247 Surface
Quartz

HU-489 Surface
Andesite

Cipolla 2005, fig.4.1

Lavallee 1985, fig.36d

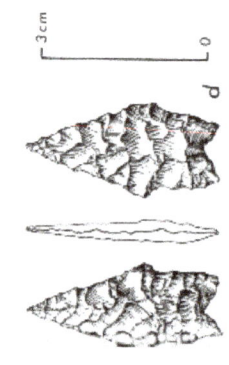

Fig. 95. Tools from *Valle de los Volcanes* – *convexo* projectile point (P4), projectile point with marginal retouche (O12), stemmed-bifurcate projectile point (O12) (drawn M. Wasilewski) with analogies from other sites

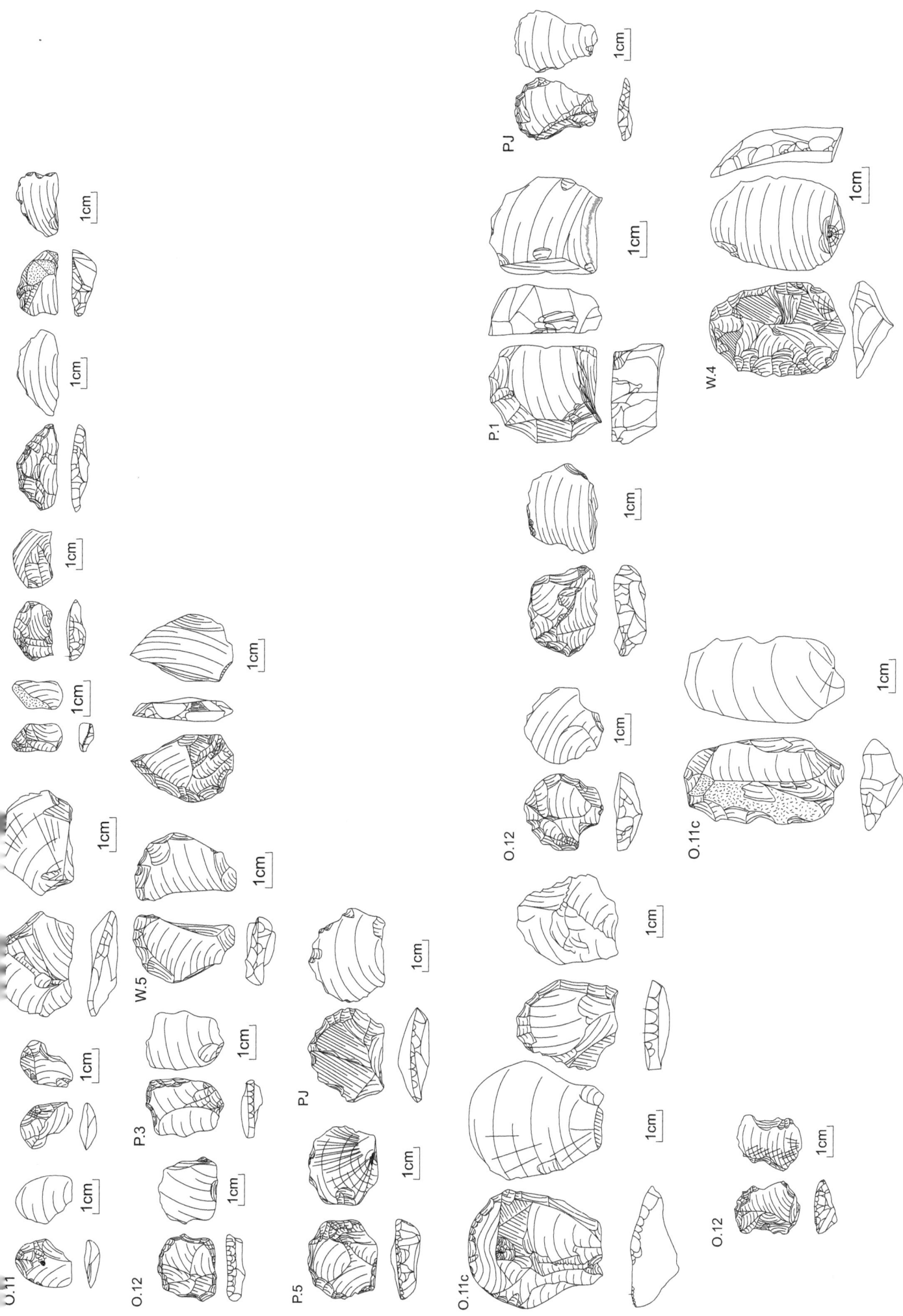

Fig. 96. Tools from Valle de los Volcanes – end-scrapers on flakes (O11, O12, P3, W5), denticulated end-scrapers (P5, PJ), semi-circular and nearly-circular end-scrapers (O11c, O12, P1, PJ), double end-scraper (O12), end-scraper on blade (O11c), end-scraper formed on a side-scraper (W4) (drawn M. Wasilewski)

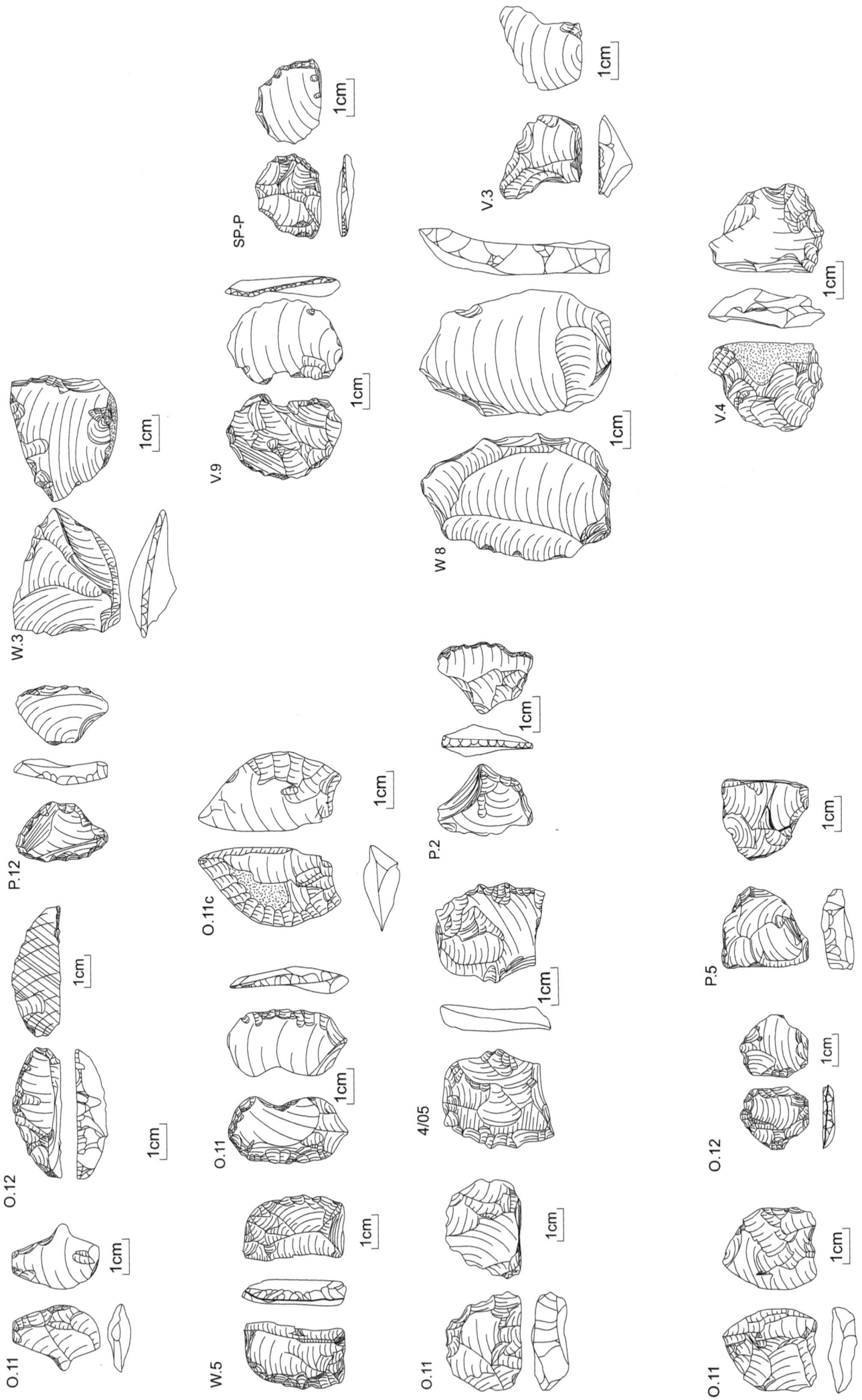

Fig. 97. Tools from Valle de los Volcanes – side-scrapers (O11, O12, P12, W3), knifes (W5, O11c, O11), *raclettes* (V9, SP-P), denticulated tools (O11, 4/05, P2), backed piece on flake (W8), truncated blade (V3), *pieces esquilles* (O11, O12, P5) tools with initial retouch (V4) (drawn M. Wasilewski)

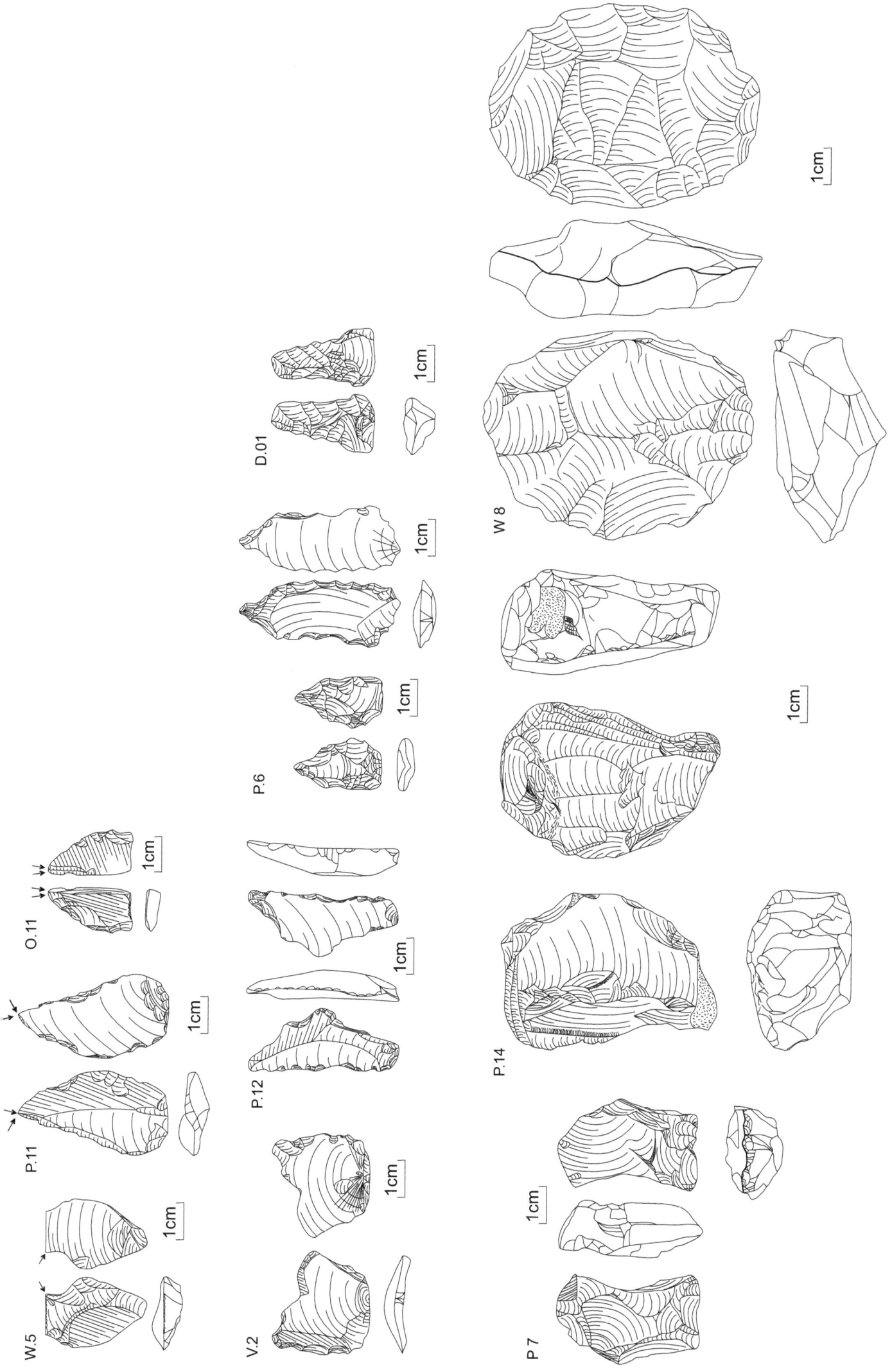

Fig. 98. Tools from Valle de los Volcanes – burins: truncation (W5), dihedral (P11) and a single blow (O11), perforators (V2, P12, P6), *perforador de muleta* (D01). Cores (P7, P14, W8) (drawn M. Wasilewski)

seen in this fact, most likely, other than a superficial similarity, however it is worth mentioning this in light of the small number of analogies of this type in South America. A similar example from the territory of Peru (the Telarmachay Cave) is cited by Lavallée (1985, fig. 36d) among the atypical projectile points of the type BI. It is much smaller, however, than the projectile points from point O12. This artifact was found in the VII stratum, dated to 12 150–6050 cal B.C. Far more interesting analogies to the projectile point described appear in the Sumbay Cave (SU-2 and SU-3) in the northern part of the Arequipa Province (Departament Arequipa). They were described by Neira Avendaño (1990) as an industry so far unencountered in the southern part of Peru, which perhaps should be linked to the oldest settlement on this terrain. The author classifies the projectile points that most interest us as the Sumbay II-A, II-B and II-E types (Neira Avendaño 1990, p. 36–37; Neira Avendaño 1998, p.19). The morphological differences between the two first variants are not great, however the last of these has been invoked here as a possibility due to the incomplete preservation of the base of the artifact from the Valley of the Volcanoes. Unfortunately, the dating of the artifacts from Sumbay leaves a lot to be desired. Only two radiometric attempts were undertaken from material collected from a depth of 20–30 cm and 30–40 cm, which correspond to cultural strata 3 and 4. The dates obtained in a laboratory in Bonn are, respectively, 5310–4804 cal B.C. and 4343–3989 cal B.C. (Ziółkowski et al. 1994). The "inverted stratigraphy" draws attention in this case, as the overlying stratum (theoretically younger) yields an older date. The picture is further clouded by the fact that Neira Avendaño (i.e. 1990) quotes completely different dates: for stratum 3– 3400 ±90 B.C., for stratum 4 – 4210 ±120 B.C.

The confusion mentioned in the question of chronology has all the less significance for us, given that on the site studied by Neira Avendaño, no clear, temporal, typological-technical variation was noticeable in the projectile points. What is more, a series of types appears in all four or at least in three of the oldest cultural strata (i.e. Sumbay II-A; Neira Avendaño 1990). We must therefore limit ourselves to the statement that artifacts of this kind should be dated to at least 5800 cal B.C. Many projectile points of a similar character come from the surface findings in the southern Peruvian puna (altiplano), from the vicinity of Lake Titicaca (Klink & Aldenderfer 2005), and also from sites situated further to the south in present-day Chile and Argentina (i.e. Tambillo, Englefield; Szykulski 2005). Such tools, morphologically corresponding to Sumbay II-B, Klink & Aldenderfer are grouped in type 3F (2005, fig. 3.4K-L).

Recently, several artifacts from Lake Titicaca have also been publicized (Cipolla 2005, fig. 4.1). They are similar to the Sumbay II-E type (and thus they have a straight base) and were described as type 4G, which is a reference to the classification of Klink & Aldenderfer (2005). An additional feature that attracts attention in comparison to the artifact from the Valley of the Volcanoes is the raw material used in their production. Just as in the case of the O12 projectile point, this is andesite. According to the author's determinations, this type of projectile point should be linked to the period of around 4900–3000 cal B.C. (Cipolla 2005).

Analogies to all the types of projectile points described above can also be successfully sought on more distant terrains. It suffices to mention the sites of Inti-Huasi (western Argentina), where there appear small, triangular projectile points with a concave base, Cuchipuy (central Chile) – several-centimeter projectile points with a stem, or Los Toldos and Cueva de Fell (Patagonia), where triangular projectile points with a flat and slightly convex base have been found (Schobinger 1988). Also to the north of the studied terrains, we find a series of similarities, such as the already mentioned projectile point of the bifurcated base type (Southeastern USA), and, also coming from these same terrains, triangular projectile points with a flat base of the types Copena Triangular, Madison as well as concave – Levanna (Fiedel 1992, Justice 1995, Hanna 2007). However, it seems that multiplication of such comparisons without the support of evidence for contacts between particular regions has little substantial value and therefore shall be omitted here. This viewpoint is all the more appropriate, given that even typological analogies of stone industry between relatively close terrains of today's northern and southern Peru are treated by many authors with great caution or are even rejected (i.e. Klink & Aldenderfer 2005).

Among the remaining tools, end-scrapers and their fragments dominate (22 pieces; Fig. 96). Most were formed on flakes (an exception is the non-obsidian end-scraper from O11). Among flake-based end-scrapers, one can find the so-called denticulated end-scrapers (P5, PJ; grattoir á front denticulé), which are recalled sometimes in the literature concerning the New World (for example, Lavallée 1985, Ginter & Kozłowski 1990). Moreover, it is possible to distinguish semi-circular and nearly-circular end-scrapers, a double end-scraper and an end-scraper formed on a side-scraper. However because this type of tool is not considered to be chronologically conclusive, and typologies are based on very different indicators (for example, size of the tool, shape of the tool, character of the retouch, etc.), reference to the typology (comparison) of end-scrapers developed at other sites has been omitted.

The rest of the collection is comprised of three cores (Fig. 98) and 26 tools and 23 retouched flakes. Among them, there have been distinguished: five perforators (Fig. 98) (V2, P6, P12, D01), including one with a very characteristic shape (D01), a so-called perforador de muleta[46], (Neira Avendaño 1990, Neira Avendaño 1998, Kaulicke 2000); while another was formed most likely on a small, used or unsuccessful geometric projectile point (P6); four side-scrapers (O11, O12, P12; Fig. 97) including one double convergent (W3); three burins (Fig. 98): truncation (W5), dihedral (P11) and a single blow (O11); three knives[47] (O11, O11c, W5; Fig. 97); three denticulated tools (O11, 4/05, P2; Fig. 97); three pieces esquilles (O11, O12, P5; Fig. 97); two raclettes (V9, SP-P; Fig. 97); a backed piece on flake (W8; Fig.97); a truncated blade (V3; Fig. 97); as well as a tool with initial retouch (V4; Fig. 97). The above-mentioned tools are not chronologically diagnostic, with the exception of the pieces esquilles which are sometimes considered to be characteristic for the Formative Period, although they are not a sufficient indicator (Ginter & Kozłowski 1990). The confirmed, coexisting ways of processing raw materials of stone (flaking technique, *pieces esquilles* technique and bifacial retouch) can be a premise for excluding paleoindian origins of the sites encountered. We possess, however, stonger chronological evidence (*projectile point cross dating*), which shall be discussed in the next chapter.

3. SUMMARY AND CONCLUSIONS

All of the research and analyses carried out enable concrete and interesting conclusions to be drawn, despite the seemingly poor material. Above all, among the 45 described points with obsidians, 16 are undoubtedly archaeological sites, and another 10 can likely be counted among this category, 7 are outcrops, and 12 are loose findings. Therefore, nearly 2/3 of the locations inventoried are connected with human activity on the terrain of the Valley of the Volcanoes. Most sites are found on the Pampa Jararanca and in the upper segments of the valleys descending from it. Below the present-day city of Chilcaymarca (around 3800 m a.s.l.), they are a rarity. Based on this, it may be concluded that obsidian was used mainly by groups of hunters, and later by pastoral people, but was not included in the supply of raw materials of the agricultural society in the Valley of the Volcanoes[48]. This was due not only to the location of natural outcrops of this rock (more than 4000 m a.s.l.) beyond reach of the farmers[49], but also to the character of the raw material itself and the way it is used. For it is a fragile (brittle) material and when it can be replaced with something else (for example, the andesite lavas that are common in the valley, silica rocks, perhaps wood, bone and in the end metal) it becomes almost completely useless in agricultural work. Small fragments found in the vicinity of the city of Andagua (points 1 and N–S) can possibly be treated as evidence for the existence of local occurrences of obsidian, because under the lavas of the Andagua formation, there occur layers of tuffs (most likely Alpabamba). Despite systematic searches, however, no outcrops of obsidian were found. They could be small, buried or completely eroded[50].

The Alpabamba tuff formation, in which the described obsidian areas were formed, appears not only in the most studied, upper part of the Cotahuasi Valley. Pieces of tuff are described, besides this, in the extensive area from Ayacucho in the northwest to Chivay in the southeast (as a rule, more than 3900 m a.s.l.). Pampa Jararanca is, according to expectations, part of the band of these acidic sediments, which continue further in the direction of the mine and the municipality of Arcata and then Chivay. Thus it is not surprising that there is volcanic glass present at some points of this region. According to field determinations, the places where vitrified silica occur in the Alpabamba formation are, as a rule, connected with the younger magma intrusions that surely caused the re-heating and partial melting of overlying sediments. Such a situation is observed at Cerro Haucahuire, Cerro Sayacata, Mistisa Palca, Quebrada Ushpa Corral and, above all, Cerro Aljajahua and Quebrada Huañajahua. Precisely in this last case, the rhyolite domes[51] (laccoliths(?)) that are somewhat younger than the tuffs discussed, are most visible in contact with rocks of the Alpabamba formation.

The instrumental tests conducted and the character of points that were surveyed allow for the unequivocal statement that the obsidian that predominates on the archaeological sites comes from the Alca 1 type deposit (46 cases, or 74.19%) and deposits of related origins described as Groups 2 and 3 (4 cases, or 6.45 %). However, because natural occurrences of obsidian of the Alca 1 type and other Alca subtypes (Groups 3 and 4; 9 cases, or 14.52%) were discovered at the same time on the studied terrain, one might suspect that the society inhabiting the upper part of the Valley of the Volcanoes used not only raw material brought in from the Cotahuasi Valley, but that tool production depended also to some extent on local material. While the deposits of the latter were less numerous and of poorer quality, they were not completely useless. Confirmation of this hypothesis is at the very least point W2 (Cerro Sayacata in the *puna* zone), which is located immediately next to an outcrop and can likely be classified as an archaeological site. Moreover, we can find analogies to the opinion expressed here in the literature on this subject. Describing the Puzolana obsidian deposit in the Ayacucho Departament, Richard L. Burger and Michael D. Glascock presume the possibility of exploitation of local raw materials, mainly in the Paleoindian and Preceramic periods, but also later, even if they appeared in lesser or technologically inferior forms (Burger & Glascock 2000, Burger *et al.* 2000).

The greatest discovery is the new types of obsidians, the existence of which has been proved on the terrain of the Valley of the Volcanoes (with proposed names Group 1, Group 5 and Group 6). While the latter two are represented by individual fragments of rocks, this is exclusively the result of the need to limit the number of samples analyzed from particular points. Group 5 is connected with an archaeological site (point P4), just as Group 6 (point W2, which is simultaneously an outcrop). The largest and thus the most interesting, Group 1 (5 cases, or 8.06%), is mainly outcrops and colluvials with obsidians (points V5-6, V7). As already mentioned, this type of obsidian also appeared on a nearby archaeological site (point V4). All of these facts testify to the exploitation, at least in a limited scope, of local deposits of volcanic glass by human populations living in the valley and on the plateau. Also, deposits of other types of stone materials (see the Appendices), different varieties of chalcedony rock and lavas whose outcrops are located both in the Valley of the Volcanoes itself, as well as in several side valleys, served for the production of tools.

In the end, it is worth pointing out the complete lack of stone material (including, in particular, obsidian) from Chivay. This situation could testify to the lack of contacts or lack of need for such contacts between human groups inhabiting these regions that are, after all, in close proximity. Difficult communication, and what follows from this – transportation problems, could also come into play, making the import of raw materials impossible or unprofitable[52] (the Alca deposits are found at a distance of 2–3 days' walk from Pampa Jararanca, without the need to overcome large elevations). This fact is interesting insofar as nearly all the obsidians on sites from the preceramic period in the Arequipa Department come precisely from the Chivay deposits (Burger *et al.* 2000). The studies conducted, therefore,

Fig. 99. Obsidian stone pavement created in the puna zone, on the border of the Ayacucho and Apurimac Departaments (phot. M. Wasilewski)

give the next reason to support the claim for a clear border running through the region of Colca Canyon (or the Canyon itself) already in the preceramic period. Its character could be manifold (geographical, cultural, ethnic, social) and is impossible to define within this work.

Moreover, both the use of mediocre-quality, but hyper-local raw materials (as opposed to the excellent deposits of Alca and Chivay), as well as the rather early exploitation of obsidian itself[53] (see below) is a confirmation of the already noted and described (for example, Lynch 1980, Rick 1980) small mobility of hunter-gatherers living in the *puna* zone. This was surely caused by the dependency of these groups on the reluctant-to-move, but very predictable herds of camelids (vicugna). Some researchers also believe that, because of this, between them no seasonal migration of human groups was necessary at all within the climatic-elevation zones of the Andes (for example, Rick 1980).

All of the archaeological sites described are surface ones. This is a common situation on the terrains of the Andes (Burger *et al.* 2000, Klink & Aldenderfer 2005). It is connected with the climatic, geomorphological and geological conditions that dominate in this area, in which sediment accumulation is very limited. Especially on the plateaux in the *puna* zone, where fluvial transport is minimal, traces of human activity are basically not covered with overlay in general. Moreover, the winds that blow there cause the removal of fine material that comes from the weathering of the surrounding slopes, exposing heavier rock fragments (including obsidian artifacts). This phenomenon, very char-

acteristic for dry and very dry areas, can be observed for example, in its classic form, in the mountains on the border of the Arequipa and Ayacucho provinces (Fig. 99).

In connection with the above phenomenon, one can expect – at least on some sites – a large amount of stone artifacts. Here, it suffices to cite the case of the Imata site (Cailoma Provence, Chivay District), where over 900 artifacts have been collected from the surface (Neira Avendaño 1998) or the site with the symbol O.11 described in this work (280 fragments).

It is difficult to unequivocally determine, on the basis of the lithic inventory's character, the function of the archaeological sites described. The small quantity of archaeological material collected is an obstacle. While it is tempting to prepare a tabulated comparison of the tools found and their contexts (Table 4 and Table 5), the conclusions that follow from these statistics should be treated with great reservation. When analyzing the material, the quantitative predominance of broken projectile points (36) over complete examples (15) draws attention. Unfortunately, there appears to be no essential dependency between the context in which they were found (site/loose finding/outcrop) and the fragment/s that were found (lower/middle/upper/broken tip). This could be interesting, because there sometimes exists a convergence between the type of fragments found, and the function of the site (for example, tips of projectile points that had been lodged in the body of the victim were brought to the campsite, and lower fragments remained at the place where the animal was killed, or the *killing site*; i.e. Rick

Obsidians in the Valley of the Volcanoes, Peru

Table 4
Comparison presenting the relations between the character of the inventories found in the Valley of the Volcanoes and:
1) the type of point in which they were found (archaeological site/loose finding); 2) the way projectile points from the inventory were damaged and/or preserved

Context / Inventory	Site (pieces)	Loose finding (pieces)	Whole projectile points (points/pieces)	Whole and broken projectile points (points/pieces)	Broken projectile points (points/pieces)
Only projectile points	4	2	2/2	2//3/3	2/2
Only other tools	5	4	-	-	-
Equilibrium of projectile points and other tools	7	1	3/3	1//3/11	4/4
Predominance of projectile points	3	0	0/0	1//2/3	2/5
Predominance of other tools	4	0	0/0	2//2/4	2/2

1980). In the situation presented, we can only presume a "post-use" sedimentation of projectile points, i.e. that they reached the archaeological context after their use as weapons. Perhaps production of projectile points (3 complete examples) took place at the site O11, which is indicated by the very large global amount of stone material, including small chips and flakes.

The location of most of the points recognized as sites on promontories, elevations and also level areas near waterways and perhaps paleo-lakes (Figs 27, 69, 70, 75, 100) can be treated as the strongest argument for the possibility of their preliminary classification as camps. The answer to the question as to whether we can also speak of processing places in the case of the sites found nearby the W2 and V4 deposits requires further research[54].

Because only surface sites were recorded during this research, it was impossible to obtain any radiocarbon dates. The theoretically possible dating based on the phenomenon of obsidian hydration is still not a precise method, and is even considered unreliable (at least in relation to the Holocene) due to the large margin of error (Wagner 1998, Anovitz *et al.* 1999, Hull 2001). In turn, carrying out typological

Fig. 100. Archaeological site (point O12) in the vicinity of the Panahua municipality and waterfalls. In the background, the Coropuna Volcano is visible (phot. M. Wasilewski)

Table 5

Comparison presenting the character of inventories at particular archaeological sites in the Valley of the Volcanoes (loose findings have also been taken into consideration in the table). A – triangular projectile point with a flat or slightly convex base, B – projectile points with a concave base, C – projectile points with a stem, D – pentagonal projectile points, E – large pentagonal projectile points, F – *convexo* projectile points, G – projectile points on a flake, H – projectile points with a *bifurcated base*.

	Projectil points								Projectil points fragments	Other tool and cores
	A	B	C	D	E	F	G	H		
O1-O4	1 o	-	-	1 o	-	-	-	-	1 o	-
O11	3 o	7 o	-	-	-	-	-	-	5 o + 1 ch	end-scrapers: 3 o + 3 ch, knifes: 1 o + 1 ch, side-scraper o, piece esquille o, burin o, 11 retouched flakes o
O12	-	1 ch	-	1 o	-	-	1 o	1 a	-	8 end-scrapers o, side-scraper o, piece esquille o, retouched flake o
D01	-	-	-	-	-	-	-	-	1 o	perforator o, retouched flake o
4/05	1 o	-	-	-	-	-	-	-	2 o	denticulated tool o, retouched flake o
5/05	2 o	-	1 o	-	-	-	-	-	1 o	-
P1	-	-	-	-	-	-	-	-	-	end-scraper o
P2-3	2 o	2 o	-	-	1 o	-	-	-	-	end-scraper o, denticulated tool o
P4	-	-	-	-	-	1 o	-	-	-	2 retouched flakes o
P5	-	-	-	-	-	-	-	-	-	end-scraper o, piece esquille o
P6	-	1 o	-	-	-	-	-	-	-	2 perforators o
P7	-	-	-	-	-	-	-	-	-	retouched flake o, core o
P10	1 o	-	-	-	-	-	-	-	-	-
P11	-	-	-	-	-	-	-	-	-	burin o
P12	1 o	-	1 o	-	-	-	-	-	-	side-scraper o, perforator o, 2 retouched flakes o
P14	-	1 o	-	-	-	-	-	-	-	core ch
W3	1 o	-	-	-	-	-	-	-	1 o	side-scraper o
W4	-	-	-	-	-	-	-	-	-	side-scraper-end-scraper o
W5	-	-	-	-	-	-	-	-	-	burin o, knife ch, 2 end-scrapers ch
W6-7	1 o	-	-	-	-	-	-	-	-	-
W8	-	-	-	-	-	-	-	-	-	backed piece on flake a, core a
W11-12	1 o	-	-	-	-	-	-	-	-	-
W15	-	1 o	-	-	-	-	-	-	-	-
V2	1 o	-	-	-	-	-	-	-	-	perforator o
V3	-	-	-	-	-	-	-	-	-	truncated blade o
V4	1 o	-	-	-	-	-	-	-	-	tool with initial retouche o
V8	-	1 o	-	-	-	-	-	-	-	retouched flake o
V9	1 o	-	-	-	-	-	-	-	-	raclette o
PJ	-	-	-	-	-	-	-	-	-	2 end-scrapers o, retouched flake o
SP-P	1 o	-	-	-	-	-	-	-	-	racletteo

The letters in the table indicate the raw material from which particular artifacts were made: o – obsidian, ch – chalcedony, a – andesite

analogies with sites from the coast is not considered appropriate practice (Rick 1996, Kaulicke 2000). Besides that, many of them have very broad dating (for example, Puyenca – around 15000–6730 cal B.C.; Neira Avendaño 1998), which impedes in drawing specific conclusions. It has thus been decided to resolve the problem of dating the material found on the basis of the article *A projectile point chronology for the South-Central Andean Highlands* (Klink & Aldenderfer 2005).

Many justifications for such a decision can be cited. Firstly, this is the latest work in this scope, and so the authors also take into account the latest findings and archaeological determinations that were not present in earlier studies. Secondly, the area of the Valley of the Volcanoes is geographically situated in the region to which the typology proposed in the article (Klink & Aldenderfer 2005, p.25) could apply. This is essential, insofar as the author of this present study, too, is inclined to this view (i.e. Rick 1996) of the mediocre quality of pan-continental or even superregional typological chronologies of stone projectile points. At last, thirdly, basing the work on carefully selected and scrupulously described artifacts with a certain stratigraphical context and geological dating methods (most often ^{14}C) guarantees its scientific correctness. This feature, unfortunately, is lacking in earlier studies devoted to pre-Columbian stone tools. We shall not refer here to all the proposals for classification of stone projectile points from the territory of Peru, limiting ourselves to only the two that deal to a large extent with the terrains of the Arequipa Departament.

The framework typochronology proposed by Neira Avendaño (1990) assumes that, initially, the most characteristic and numerous were the foliate-shaped projectile points and those with a fluted base (comparable to Clovis/Lindenmeier projectile points). Somewhat later, there appear rhomboid (so-called *diamond*), pentagonal and finally stemmed projectile points. All of these types were supposed to occur in the period of around 9500–6000 cal B.C. Additionally, in the period 6000–3800 cal B.C., triangular projectile points of obsidian with straight or concave bases came into use, although they are not chronologically sensitive, as they appear even up to the Late Horizon.

Burger, Chavez & Chavez (2000) treat the problem in more detail. According to these researchers, in the preceramic period (11105–9850 B.P. = around 11180–9280 cal B.C.) projectile points with a stem predominate. In its late part (around 6150–3640 B.P. = around 5050–2015 cal B.C.) there appear different types of triangular projectile points, of small dimensions as a rule (and mainly with a concave base), common in the Initial Period (3750–2750 B.P. = around 2130–900 cal B.C.) The next type, chronologically (appearing already in the Late Initial Period), is the small, hafted projectile points with a stem. In the Early Horizon (2750–2050 B.P. = around 900–50 cal B.C.) there begin to dominate projectile points with a straight base, which become increasingly long at the final part of this period. In inventories, it is still possible to encounter concave projectile points, which in the Middle Horizon (1400–1050 B.P. = around 650–995 cal A.D.) once more become dominant in tool groups. However, they undergo a clear miniaturization, and are accompanied by small hafted projectile points with a stem and a straight base. The miniaturization and frequency of these types is connected with the spread of the use of the bow in Huari and Tiahuanaco. In the times of the Incas (Late Horizon, 1476–1532 A.D.), projectile points with a concave base, often formed on flakes and thus with an incomplete retouch of the surface (for example, from Sillustani) become the most characteristic.

Klink & Aldenderfer (2005), relating their typology to radiocarbon dates, refer in their conclusions to findings that have not yet been dated or that have been dated uncertainly. Such a structure of the work enables us to gain wider comparative material and preliminary dating of projectile points found in the Valley of the Volcanoes. The typology was based on the idea of series and type. The series, in the au-

thors' definition, is a "broad category defined by a general set of shared attributes," while the type is a "series subdivision that is delineated by differences in other characteristics *i.e.* essential attributes a point must exhibit to be classified into" (Klink & Aldenderfer 2005, p.27). Five series have been distinguished:

1. spine-shouldered forms, among which two types are distinguished: diamond/foliate (1A) and pentagonal (1B). This series is characteristic for the period 10000–8000 B.P. (around 9500–7000 cal B.C.). No such varieties have been confirmed among the artifacts from the Valley of the Volcanoes.

2. angular to round-shouldered unstemmed forms, among which three types are distinguished: foliate (2A), diamond to rhomboid (2B) and pentagonal (2C). Type 2A is characteristic for the turn of the Early and Middle Archaic (9000–7000 B.P. = around 8250–5850 cal B.C.), 2B – for the late Middle Archaic (7000–6000 B.P. = around 5850–4900 cal B.C.), 2C – for the Middle Archaic (8000–6000 B.P. = around 7000–4900 cal B.C.). In the Valley of the Volcanoes there were two projectile points similar to type 2B or 2C (at point O12; Fig. 94).

3. unstemmed, unshouldered foliate forms, among which are distinguished six types: wide, contracting haft with straight base (3A), edge-modified foliates with straight to contracting haft margins (3B), expanding haft foliates (3C), contracting to parallel-sided foliates without edge modification (3D–E) and concave base lanceolate forms (3F). They are diagnostic, respectively: 3A – for the Early and Middle Archaic (10 000–6000 B.P. = around 9500–4900 cal B.C.), 3B – exclusively for the Middle Archaic (8000–6000 B.P. = around 7000–4900 cal B.C.), 3C and D for the entire Preceramic Period, 3E – for the Middle Archaic, and 3F – for the Late Archaic (6000–4400 B.P. = around 4900–3000 cal B.C.). On the studied terrain, there was also found a fragment of a projectile point which could be considered type 3F (point O12; Fig. 95). It is not entirely certain as to whether another fragment (from point P4; Fig. 95) can be attributed to type 3D.

4. stemmed forms, among which six types are distinguished: triangular-bladed, broad-stemmed forms with contracting hafts (4A), small, narrow, broad-stemmed forms with contracting hafts (4B), squat, narrow-stemmed forms with contracting hafts (4C), large, broad-stemmed forms with parallel-sided hafts (4D), elongated, narrow-stemmed forms with barbed shoulders (4E), small, broad-stemmed forms with parallel-sided hafts (4F). Types 4A and B are dated to the Early Archaic (10 000–8000 B.P. = around 9500–7000 cal B.C.), 4C – to the Formative Period (1600 cal B.C. – 400 cal A.D.), 4D and F – to the Late Archaic (6000–4400 B.P. = around 4900–3000 cal B.C.) and 4E – to the period of the Middle Horizon (1400–1050 B.P. = around 650–990/1000 cal A.D.). Type 4G – large, broad-stemmed with edges that broaden towards the bottom[55] – has been added to this classification, as well as 4H – differing from 4G in its greater stem length and a base that is convex to contracting (Cipolla 2005). The author suggests dating both types to the Late Archaic (6000–4400 B.P. = around 4900–3000 cal B.C.). Among the artifacts found during field prospecting in the Valle de los Volcanes, projectile

points that could be classified as types 4D were distinguished (from point P12 and possibly P2; Fig. 94), 4F (from point 5/05; Fig. 94).

5. unstemmed, unshouldered triangular forms, among which four types have been distinguished: ovo-triangular (5A), straight-based to convex-based triangular forms (5B), large triangular forms with concave bases (5C), small triangular forms with concave bases (5D). The authors date them: 5A – to the Final Archaic (4400–3600 B.P. = around 3000–1950 cal B.C.), 5B – from the Final Archaic to the decline of the Tiwanaku (4400–900 B.P. = around 3000 cal B.C. - 1100 cal A.D.), 5C – to the time from Final Archaic to the Formative Period (4400–1450 B.P. = around 3000 cal B.C. - 550 cal A.D.), 5D – mainly to the Late Formative Period (2850–1450 B.P. = around 1000 cal B.C. – 550 cal A.D.) although they appear in other periods too. At many sites in the Valley of the Volcanoes, there have been found projectile points of the types: 5B (points 4/05, 5/05, W3, W6, W11-12, P2, P10, P12, V2, V4, V9, O11, 16 pieces in total; Fig. 92), 5C (points O1-O4, O11, P6, P14, V8, 8 pieces in total) and 5D (points P2, P3, O11, O12, 7 pieces in total; Fig. 92).

The combinations presented here in brief, together with the typological analogies cited in Chapter II.4 reveal the following picture of the history of the Valle de los Volcanes[56]. The most common types of projectile point – triangular with a straight or slightly convex base, and triangular with a concave base – appear in the upper part of the Valley of the Volcanoes in the vicinity of Orcopampa-Sarpane, in the high, flat parts of side valleys (for example, below the Poracota Mine and near the village of Panahua), on the Pampa Jararanca and its surroundings. These types are most often dated to the Final Archaic and the Formative Period (around 3000 cal B.C. – 500/550 cal A.D.). Small (with a length < 2 cm), triangular projectile points with a concave base also appearing on these same terrains are dated to a somewhat later period, namely the Formative Period (around 1000 cal B.C. – 500/550 cal A.D.).

It is not entirely out of the question that some projectile points of larger dimensions from the triangular group with a straight base could have an earlier chronology. Specimens with a similar morphology dated to the period of the Middle/Late Archaic (around 7200–4000 cal B.C.) are cited in the works of Schroeder (*fide* Neira Avendaño 1990) and Lynch (1980). However, because the first of these examples is dated only by a distant analogy to the industry of Ayampitinense II, and the second comes from the distant Puna Junin, they should be treated with great reservation from the view of estimating the age of tools from the Valley of the Volcanoes. The triangular projectile points with a concave base from Puna Junin, dated just as early, can rather be treated as a superficial, deceptive analogy.

Several rarer specimens yield other dates. The three projectile points with a stem found in the level area below the Poracota Mine and in the vicinity of Orcopampa (including one distinguished as a separate type due to the size and width of the stem) should be linked to the Late and Final Archaic period (around 4900–1950 cal B.C.). Because they appeared together with triangular projectile points of both types, their chronology can surely by narrowed to the

Final Archaic (around 3000–1950 cal B.C.). The dating of other analogies cited in Chapter II.4 in the majority largely coincide with those mentioned, indicating however the end of the Late Archaic (around 3500–3000 cal B.C.) as the possible date of the artifacts' origins.

Also dated to the period of the Late Archaic (around 5000/4900–3000 cal B.C.) is the foliate-shaped projectile point with a bifurcated base, found on the level area in the vicinity of the Panahua village. There is, after all, agreement among most researchers in the question of such dating. Two pentagonal projectile points, of which one appeared below the Poracota Mine, and the second, once more, in the vicinity of Panahua village, are likely the oldest tools in the collection. Similar specimens are dated to the middle or late Middle Archaic (7000–5850–4900 cal B.C.). Projectile points of this type found on other terrains usually obtain similar dates, fluctuating within a range of 8000–4000 cal B.C.

A fragment of flake with an edge modified in the shape of a projectile point has no analogy in the typology of Klink & Aldenderfer (2005). It can be compared to a similar artifact from Puna Junin, dated to around 2900–500 cal B.C. (Rick 1980), but this territorially distant analogy must be treated very cautiously. Besides that, the proposed dating does not bring anything new to the chronology built on the basis of other, more certain projectile points. The last of the projectile points found with a semicircular (convergent) base, appearing over the whole Preceramic period, is not a good chronological indicator. Unfortunately, it is impossible to perceive a connection between the chronology of stone tools and the degree and type of raw materials used, with the exception of the somewhat more popular non-obsidian materials at the younger sites in the middle part of the valley.

At the sites of the area discussed, no other traces of human activity besides the stone material have been found. There is a complete lack of ceramic, and any organic raw materials have certainly disintegrated or been consumed. Similarly, it should be assumed that at least some of the tools treated as curated were removed from the sites already by the time of their establishment[57]. Also later, artifacts resting on the surface might have been re-used or simply collected (which local people have been doing to this day). At the same time, it must be remembered that mobile groups of hunters, and later herders, did not build durable housing structures. A certain exception is point V3 (in Quebrada Paco), at which there has been described a curved row of unshaped rocks (a rock "wall") with a radius of around 2.5–3 m, surrounding part of the site from the side of the river and the opening of a ravine. The purpose of this structure is not clear. The diameter, however, might suggest that the structure served rather as the reinforcement of the base of a fence/screen protecting a camp (?) from the wind, or demarcating the zone of camp activity (compare, for example, Lavallée 1985, 2000), rather than as a corral. The lack of a larger number of boulders that could have come from knocking down a higher wall additionally negates the possibility of recognizing this structure as the remains of farmsteads that are common on these terrains for domestic animals, or obstacles serving to protect them (i.e. located in

Fig. 101. Flake made from andesite lava of the Andahua formation (phot. M. Wasilewski)

front of precipices). Similar, but somewhat larger (8–10 m in diameter), oval structures have been recorded in the area of study (at point D01). It cannot be ruled out that, in this case as well, we can accept an analogical explanation.

To recapitulate, the material possessed does not allow us to say, for now, anything more than that the archaeological sites located on the terrain were places where hunter-gatherers – and later, herders – had stayed since at least the turn of the Middle and Late Archaic (around 4900 cal B.C.). Certain circumstances (pentagonal projectile points) can suggest earlier, lasting from at least the second half of the Middle Archaic (5850 cal B.C.) visits of man in the Valley of the Volcanoes, connected mainly with the presence, amount and mobility of herds of tarucas, guanacos and vicugnas in conditions of a drying climate (Aldenderfer 2000). Perhaps some of these traces were obliterated by volcanic activity. Also drawing attention is the fact that the potentially oldest sites are situated in places that were excellently supplied with water (today's Panahua icefalls, wetlands and the springs of Poracota). However, more intensive exploitation of the valley and adjacent *puna* zones undoubtedly lasted through the entire Final Archaic and Formative Period (around 3000 cal B.C. – 500/550 cal A.D.). In precisely this period (from around 3800 cal B.C.), the climate became cooler (Aldenderfer 2000), but also more humid, which encouraged the development of fauna, and as a result also the expansion and success of hunter-gatherers and later herders on the terrains that earlier had been dry.

4. APPENDICES

4.1. Non-obsidian rock materials in the Valley of the Volcanoes

Of the total number of nearly 1000 fragments collected (raw materials and artifacts), obsidian comprises 78.06 % (779 pieces), and other raw materials – 21.94% (219 pieces). However, because there have been documented on the terrain of the Valley of the Volcanoes both outcrops of such rocks, as well as tools and flakes made from them (sometimes accompanying obsidian ones), this appendix has been included in this work to make it more complete. Although no chemical analysis was carried out on the other raw materials collected besides obsidian, it can be justifiably be presumed that the flakes and tools present on the sites were made from local rocks, whose deposits in the valley have been described.

From the perspective of petrography, among the non-obsidian material found on archaeological sites (points 3-4, 6-7, 8, O.10, O.11, 1/05, 5/05, P1, P4, P5, P10, P12,

Fig. 102. Examples of raw materials and flakes from siliceous rocks from the Valley of the Volcanoes: a) white chalcedony from point O10; b) green, white, gray-white layered chalcedony and colorless quartz from point O9; c) reddish, black, honey, brown, white and green chalcedony flakes (point O9); d) white-honey chalcedony flake (point U1); e) obsidian flake and red-white and black chalcedony (point W2); f) red chalcedony flake with white spots from point W2 (phot. M. Wasilewski)

P13, P14, U1, W2, W5, W6-7, W8, V2, V3, V9, SP-P, PJ) chalcedony and andesite predominate. The latter rock comes from the lava streams of the Andahua formation (Figs 5, 101) that litter the floor of the Valley of the Volcanoes. This material is thus available nearly everywhere, and is also found on all archaeological sites in the form of a substratum, natural fragments and sometimes artifacts. The rock is black in color, with a porphyritic texture (matrix with visible protocrystals of plagioclases and/or zeolites) and uneven fracture (Fig. 101). It is marked by great hardness and durability, and its freshly-made edges are sharp. It is difficult to prepare more delicate or technically more so-

phisticated tools from this material, but products made from it are very durable.

The raw material described in this work as chalcedony is a silica rock that appears in the upper part of the Valley of the Volcanoes in the form of veins, strata, talus and colluvia. It is characterized by a conchoidal or uneven fracture, great hardness (around 6.5 on the Mohs scale) and significant color variation (white, cream or beige, honey, yellow, green, red, brown, black, gray, black-and-white spotted, and also multi-colored, layered varieties have been encountered; Fig. 102), which testifies to the numerous and various admixtures contained in these rocks. Here, we have taken the

Fig. 103. Outcrops of chalcedony veins in the formation of the Tacaza Group: a) point 2/05; b) point 3/05 (phot. M. Wasilewski)

convention of calling all silica formations chalcedony – from the name of the main mineral component. This is justified by the fact that all of these rocks arose as a result of silification and recrystallization.

Features (for example, cleavage) indicate that it is not made of opal. Thus it would not be entirely appropriate to call these formations bedded cherts, jasper, chert, radiolarite or even chalcedonite, all of which are, by definition, rocks of sedimentary and often biogenic origin. There are also insufficient grounds in this case to apply the detailed names of silificated rock, such as helleflint. Thus, the alternative is either to use the developed name "volcanogenic silica rock" or else to refer to their main component and the description "chalcedony." For practical reasons, the second option was chosen, even though it may inspire certain controversies.

The chalcedonies described came about as a result of the transformation of tuffs in the Tacaza-Orcopampa Group (case O.8 and O.9). Just as in the case of obsidian deposits, the direct causal factor was intrusion of magma rocks. Perhaps, however, some of the deposits are syngenetic, or arose already at the moment of the creation of some sediments of the formations mentioned – this mainly concerns ignimbrite streams of Tacaza-Orcopampa (case 2/05 and 3/05; Fig. 103). Silica formations of this type (or partly crystallized ones) arise at lower temperatures or in the case of slower cooling of heated rocks than in the case of obsidians. All the outcrops found appear in the slopes of the main valley or to the east of it (with the exception of point P15).

Both the accessibility and abundance of deposits of andesite lavas, as well as chalcedony, should be described as great or very great. It is surely due to this that we find the common presence of such rocks and products made from them on archaeological sites in the Valley of the Volcanoes. Their popularity compensated for their interior technical parameters with respect to obsidian processing. For these are stones with poorer cleavage (andesites) or creating other processing problems (chalcedony). The latter often have interior flaws, fractures or different interbeddings which make it difficult to obtain larger flakes and shavings or to make tools. However, if a tool was made from such a raw material, then it would surely be more durable than one made of obsidian. This fact might explain their somewhat greater popularity at agricultural sites, where obsidian artifacts are basically absent (points 3-4, 6-7, 8). Besides this, the raw materials described here were available directly to farmers (within 1 day's walk). Taking into consideration the coexistence of both raw materials at many points[58], it may also be assumed that the aesthetic aspect (the color of chalcedony) was not without influence on the fact of its use both in hunter and pastoral societies.

4.2. Other archaeological sites located during field surveys in the Valley of the Volcanoes

Besides "obsidian" and "non-obsidian" surface sites, more attention should certainly be devoted to two stone structures at Pampa Jararanca (point W8, Fig. 104). These are two artificial, 3/4-circles, composed of stones (partly still standing on end, sunken into the ground (?)), with a radius of 5–6 m each. They are adjacent to a small rock elevation on a flat area of the *pampa*, with their greatest bulge pointing northward (N, with a slight deflection to the N–N–E). They are mentioned here, as they appear deceptively similar to of one of the circles from the Sillustani site in the vicinity of Lake Titicaca (Fig. 105). The latter were first described in the second half of the XIX century by E. George Squier, an American traveler and naturalist, as "sun circles" (Squier 1870). It is thought – as Squier had already suggested – that they could be an element of a sun cult, connected with pre-Inca times. They can likely be linked to the idea of *Intihuatana*, or the hitching post of the sun. However, the suggestion of a similarity between the two structures (from Sillustani and Pampa Jararanca) requires decidedly closer examination before it can be recognized as likely.

Fig. 104. Stone structures encountered at Pampa Jararanca **a**) eastern circle (northeast); **b**) western circle (southwest) (phot. M. Wasilewski)

Obsidians in the Valley of the Volcanoes, Peru

Fig. 105. Sun circles at the Sillustani site in the vicinity of Lake Titicaca (phot. M. Wasilewski)

Fig. 106. Site with rock art in the Valley of the Volcanoes, above Laguna Mamacocha, vicinity of Ayo (phot. M. Wasilewski)

Another atypical site is the point with rock art (Fig. 106). It is located in the immediate vicinity of Lake Mamacocha (Ayo District). Today, there is no direct access to the site, because as a result of the breaking away of part of the rock wall (and path), it is situated at a height of around 15 m above the ground. The representations were made in reddish–brown colors and occupy around 1–1.5 m^2. They depict animals (camelids and/or deer) as well as geometric patterns (lines and ladders). The drawings are very schematic, the outlines of animals were conveyed with simple lines, and in three cases the trunk is marked by a thickened smudge of color. Rock art known from the territorially closest sites (Pintasayoc, Sumbay; Fig. 107) has a completely different character (Neira Avendaño 1990). Representations of "full" silhouettes of animals and humans, sometimes arranged into scenes, dominate in them. Stylistically much closer, however, are the paintings from the sites Amaitira waiq'o, Pentasqaqa, Qarwaqaqa, Qotallany (all in the Carabaya Province, Puno Departament; Fig. 108a–g) and more distant ones such as Canchanhuanca-Yanacocha (Daniel Alcides Carrion Province, Pasco Departament; Fig. 108h). Unfortunately, most Peruvian representations of rock art do not have absolute dates. In a totally preliminary manner, based on the perspective of stylistic development in this art (Guffroy 1999), one might suppose that the paintings from the Valley of the Volcanoes are younger than 3000/3500 B.C. That would coincide with the dates from sites in the upper reaches of the valley and could be a premise for confirming the presence of human groups

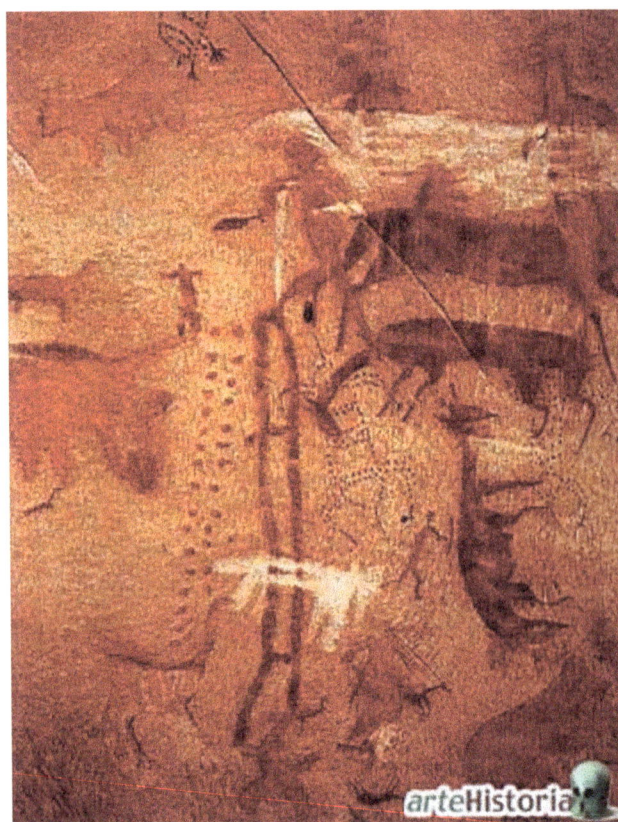

Fig. 107. Example of rock paintings from the grottoes of Sumbay (source: ArteHistoria)

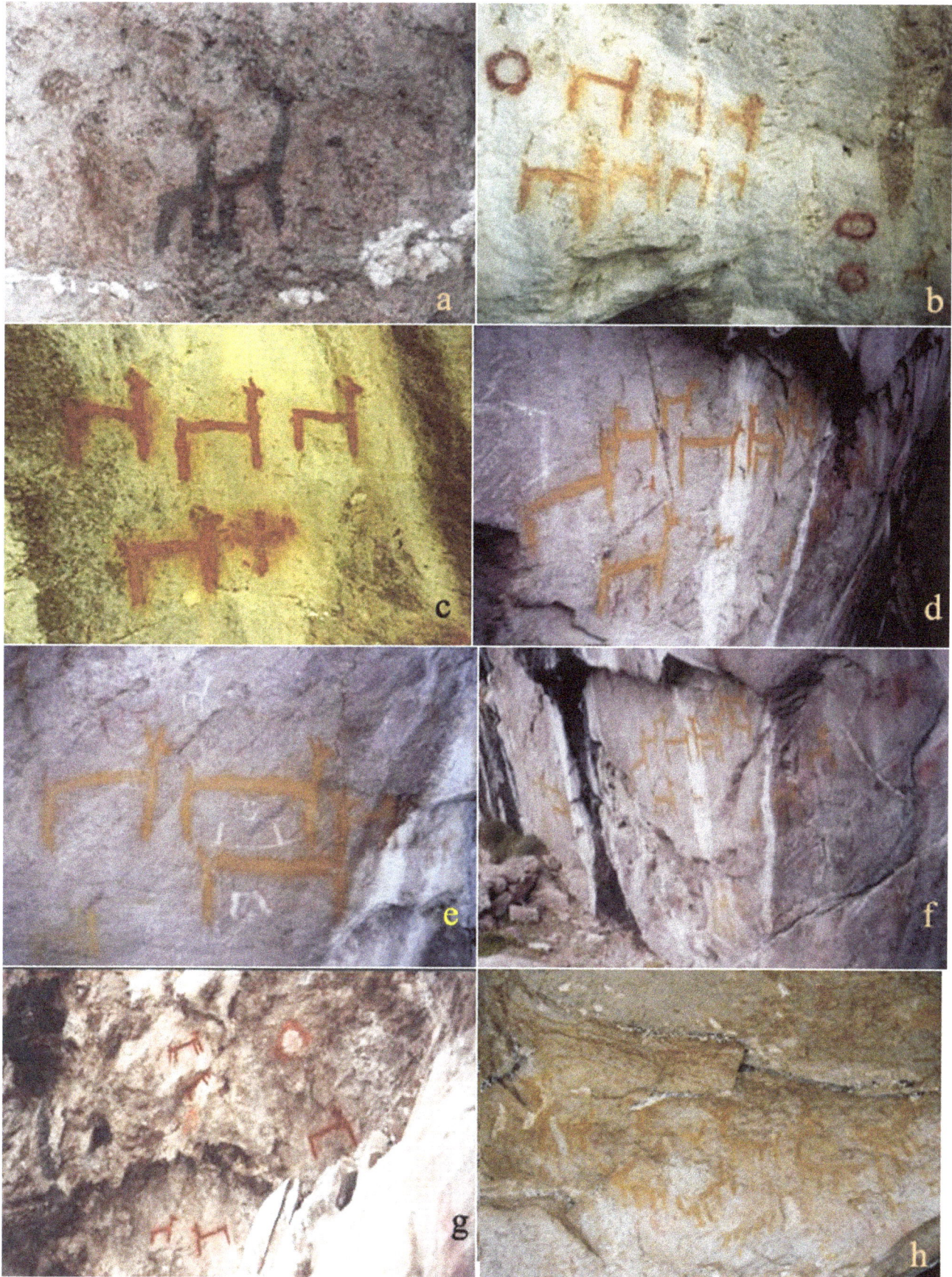

Fig. 108. Examples of rock art from the Carabaya Province, Puno Departament: **a**) Amaitira waiq'o; **b, c**) Pentasqaqa; **d–f**) Qarwaqaqa; **g**) Qotallany; **h**) from the Daniel Alcides Carrion Province, Pasco Departament, Canchanhuanca-Yanacocha site (phot. A. Quispe)

in the lower parts as well, where other traces have been obliteratede by volcanic activity. However, it cannot be completely ruled out that the drawings found in the Valley of the Volcanoes come from later times, perhaps even historical.

Acknowledgements

First of all I would like to thank professor Mariusz Ziółkowski, PhD, whose permission let me do the research under his archaeological concession in Condesuyos Province. He was also the person who during our discussions first proposed the idea of this subject. I must express my gratitude to all my colleagues from *Polish Scientific Expedition Peru – Parco Nacional Colca*, and in particular to professor Andrzej Paulo, PhD. All of them always encourage and adhere me during the realisation of this difficult task. Last but not least I would like to thank professor Jan Chochorowski, PhD, for his confidence and financial help during the laboratory analysis. Without kindness and understanding of this people the project won't be implemented.

Notes

1. Most rivers and streams change their names every few kilometers. What is more, the information shown on maps does not always agree with the actual local name.
2. This name refers to Mother-Sea, the pre-Columbian goddess of surface waters.
3. Other biotopes described in this zone (for example, lake shores) are not observed on the studied terrain.
4. According to some authors, this name is also used to describe species of grass from the genera *Festuca* and *Calamagrostis* (Pearsall 1980).
5. An animal the size and shape of a camel, with a nose elongated to form a small trunk (similar to that of contemporary tapirs). It belonged to the now extinct Order *Litopterna* and the family *Macrauchenidae*.
6. Throughout the entire work, the author has made efforts to give exclusively or additionally calibrated dates. Working (approximate) calculations have been prepared, based mainly on the work of Ziółkowski *et al.* (1994) and Walanus & Goslar (2004).
7. In the uncovered deposits described, besides gold there are several other metals (i.e. silver) which, however, for economic reasons are not an object of exploitation (they are not extracted from the ore). In past centuries, gold deposits were also accessible on the surface, hence their widespread exploitation.
8. One must remember, however, that a certain inconsistency in names on geological maps of Peru, as well as the lack of correlation of particular outcrops (particularly those found on separate pages of a map) and also different views of researchers means that the description "obsidian-bearing" is likewise applied to the Miocene formations of the Barroso Group (Burger *et al.* 1998b) or to the entire Tacaza Group (Burger *et al.* 1998a). These formations are also made of volcanic rock, mainly tuffs, ignimbrites, dacites and andesites, and dated to 6-1 Ma and 30-18 Ma, respectively (Paulo 2008).
9. According to the terminology proposed by Cardich, these are the Magapata phase (15 500-13 000 B.P.), the Aguamiro interphase (13 000-12 000 B.P.) and the Antarraga phase (12 000-11 000/10 500 B.P.) of Lauricocha glaciation (Cardich *fide* Lavallée 1985).
10. There is no full agreement as to the beginning of this period. Some researchers place it even 1000 years later (around 3950 cal B.C.) at the end of the Holocene climate optimum (see Aldenderfer 1998).
11. El Niño-Southern Oscillation (ENSO) – periodic changeability of the climate in the inter-tropical territories near the Pacific, connected with the ocean currents called *el Niño* and *la Niña*. It occurs every 5-7 years (although some researchers point out its greater aperiodicity (Bruhns 1996)), causing, for example, violent rains on the South American coast and droughts on the islands of Oceania.
12. Broader treatment of the subject of the quantity of supplies, their availability and "caloric value" and of problems connected with these questions can be found, for example, in: Lynch 1980, Rick 1980, Lavallée 1985, Aldenderfer 1998 and others.
13. As far as at least these dates are concerned, there exists among archaeologists a general agreement. At the same time, the author does not negate here the reliability of some older sites in South America, but omits them from the discussion as extraneous to the topic of this work, and requiring the citation of a series of arguments and explanations.
14. It is believed that more permanent camps such as these should be expected usually in caves, somewhat lower than the *puna* zone. So far, however, no such examples have been found in the Valley of the Volcanoes.
15. The domestication process was, however, very slow and occurred at different times in different areas. In the Pachamachay cave, hunting dominated all the way up to around 1600 B.C., while in the Telarmachay cave 100 km away, evidence of domestication has been dated to 3800 B.C.
16. In some cases, seasonal settlement of particular zones by the same group of people was also possible, in connection with the annual changes in the amount of precipitation. Such migration in the course of a year undoubtedly influenced the enrichment of the group's inventory and skills, and could have served as the basis for future specialization.
17. Both researchers limited themselves to describing sites known to the locals, with remains of architecture, located in the most easily-accessible, central part of the Valley.
18. Dr. Luis Augusto Belan Franco – Museo Arqueologico Universidad Católica de Santa Maria in Arequipa; prof. dr. hab. Mariusz Ziółkowski – Archaeological Institute, History Faculty of Warsaw University.
19. *Chullpa* are round or rectangular tombs in the shape of towers. They were built of different materials (dried bricks, stones and shaped stone blocks) mainly in the Altiplano zone, from the Late Intermediate Period.
20. These objects (mainly projectile points and their fragments) are kept in a nearby school that fulfils the role of "museum." However, because the collection has not been put in any sort of order, it is not known where, exactly, the artifacts originated (some have been brought in from outside the Valley of the Volcanoes, as for example, the projectile point of red chalcedony in fig. 34), and artifacts are dispersed and added (for example, worse or uglier specimens are "exchanged" for prettier ones) without endeavoring to describe them. An additional obstacle was the unusually short time that could be devoted to getting acquainted with the collection. However, even this superficial inspection is enough to confirm that among the collected artifacts there are neither any projectile points that differ completely from those found by the author, nor ones that are especially interesting from a chronological standpoint.
21. The object, to a large extent dismantled (or destroyed), has a diameter of around 2.5-3 m and presently a height of around 1.5-2 m; it is made of flat stones – plates.
22. The "*abuelo* cult" is a cult of ancestors (most often mummies), manifested in the bringing of gifts and caring for the deceased. It is considered that this "grandfather" (Spanish – *abuelo*), "in

exchange," takes care of the local people and their herds.

23. The plans to create a National Park in part of the Valley of the Volcanoes and Colca Canyon will undoubtedly influence the situation for the worse in this scope. This project is, in spite of it all, a useful, joint Polish-Peruvian idea, but will compel the undertaking of decisive archaeological salvage work. The author is participating in its preparation in the role of geoarchaeologist.

24. The Paccareta site (Pacarita, Pajareta) should be associated with this period; in relation to it, Neira Avendaño (1990) expresses the view that the projectile points found there resemble blades of the Lindenmeier type (Folsom complex). However, let us add that this is, for now, a rather isolated opinion, and these projectile points rather resemble territorially closer artifacts from the Asana site, from the Asana Phase IV/Muruq'uta (6650-4900 cal B.C.) (Aldenderfer 1998, fig. 7.17 c-d) or some of the projectile points of Sumbay (e.g. Sumbay II-B; Neira Avendaño 1990, fig. on page 36).

25. The chronological framework of particular periods is mainly from Burger et al. 2000. The Preceramic Period is also called the Archaic Period and is divided into an Early (11 000-8000 B.P. = around 11 050-7050 cal B.C.), Middle (8000-6000 B.P. = around. 7050-4900 cal B.C.) and Late (6000-4000 B.P. = around 4900-2550 cal B.C.) (Aldenderfer 1998). One should remember that, to date, there has been no complete agreement in the question of the duration and even the names of particular periods in the prehistory of South America.

26. The basis of such dating was the appearance, in lower strata of the Arcata site, of projectile points attributed by the discoverer to the Ayampitinense II Period.

27. There are known examples of traces of later developmental phases of Nazca from Cotahuasi Valley – the Allway site (Neira Avendaño 1998).

28. Some researchers see in this fact even the influence of the Late/Final Wari (Huari) culture on the territory of the Valley of the Volcanoes (Neira Avendaño 1990, Neira Avendaño 1998).

29. Sometimes identified with the Virgin Mary.

30. The initial idea for considering the problem of obsidian on this terrain was suggested to the author by prof. dr. hab. M. Ziółkowski.

31. One should remember that obsidian is a nondurable form and undergoes quick, from the perspective of geological time, weathering – hydration reaction. It is precisely because of this that no deposits of this rock older than 10 Ma are known, and most are younger than 100 ka. Thus, it can be seen that the "shortness" of its life has no significance in archaeological categories, and it can be treated as an immutable source of information.

32. Prof. Dr hab. Andrzej Paulo, Department of Environmental Analysis and Cartography, Faculty of Geology, Geophysics and Environmental Protection of AGH University of Science and Technology in Cracow.

33. Compañía de Minas Buenaventura – Orcopampa.

34. Represented in this region by engineer M. Castro and engineer J. Rojas, directors of the Orcopampa mining group.

35. Samples WAS008-WAS020 came from the Alca and Chivay sources, and are not taken into consideration in the collective tables of this work. They were only an object of study for control-comparison purposes.

36. It may be recalled that for similar material-intensive projectile points of the Clovis or Folsom types in North America, the proportion of tools to flakes is reckoned to be 6:10000 (Haury et al. 1953; Fagan 2004). In the case described, one should obviously take into account the fact that they did not have to be the place of production of the tools (workshops), but rather the

killing or butchering sites, nevertheless, the predominance of tools over unshaped flakes would also be rather an anomaly. Here, in addition, it should be pointed out that frequent renewal was necessary for products made from such a brittle material, and that such objects are treatd as curated products, which should also change the proportions in favor of flakes.

37. The material was never gathered in its entirety, thus it should not be suggested in any of the cases to be a description concerning the quantity of fragments gathered for studies, included in this work.

38. The Alca deposit is one of the most important sources of obsidian in the Peruvian Andes. It was exploited from the Paleoindian Period until the Late Horizon, and for a long time was the most important place of extracting this raw material for the Cusco and Arequipa regions. The scale of extraction, following the apogee in the period of the Wari domination, clearly dropped in the Incan times. However, after the 1980s, a mine of this raw material functioned on the slopes of Cerro Aycano – the only one known in this area (Jennings & Glascock 2002).

39. Group 4 converges with it the least, however due to the small quantity of samples tested and, despite it all, a small difference in the chemical composition, it was decided not to distinguish it as a new type.

40. The remaining 13 samples were, as mentioned, a control group, originating from the Alca and Chivay deposits described in the literature.

41. Here, there also appears a new subtype of Alca – Group 2 (N-S-a = WAS023).

42. The fundamental, although in reality none too evident, difference between older and newer triangular projectile points with a concave base is the fluting of the former (Neira Avendaño 1990, Szykulski 2005). The oldest examples do not always have this feature, however (vide Rick 1980), and its absolute exclusion from newer artifacts is sometimes uncertain (vide Klink 2007).

43. Although at the Ichuña site there appear projectile points with a concave base, these are by no means projectile points of the Ichuña type. Here it is worth remembering the imprecisions present in the literature. Some authors cite projectile points of the Ichuña type as being escotados, or those with a concave base (Lynch 1980, Rick 1980, Schroeder fide Neira Avendaño 1990 and others). However, in the text of Klink & Aldenderfer (2005, p.31) there have been quoted, in extenso, original descriptions by Ravines, the creator of the term "Punta Ichuña," who most other researchers writing about such tools refer to, after all. In the work "Secuencia y cambios en los artefactos liticos del sur de Perú" (1972, Revista del Museo Nacional 38:133-185) Ravines writes: "tipo P2, Punta Ichuña (...) hojas de limbo dentado (...) de dos variedades: una con aletas diminutivas y otra sin aletas". Such a description indicates unequivocally a completely different type of projectile point – with a sharp, convergent base. It is precisely to such variants that Klink & Aldenderfer (2005) compare the Ichuña projectile points, indicating the types defined by them as 1A (foliate with hafts) and 3B (diamond-shaped without hafts) (see also Burger et al. 2000, p.282, Szykulski 2005, p.123 and fig.14). In its own way, the type discussed has already met with criticism that points out precisely the fact that it contains two completely different kinds of projectile points (Burger et al. 2000).

44. This form commonly appears, after all, in the southern part of Peru, mainly on the coast (Szykulski 2005).

45. This form of stem is sometimes described as a "stem with a concave base" (Szykulski 2005, p.112).

46. In the literature, one can encounter the idea – as interesting as it is surprising – that the artifacts described as perforadores de

muleta are in reality the stems of triangular projectile points (Szykulski 2005, p.118). Analyzing the artifact from point D01, however, we do not find evidence in support of such a statement. Moreover, it is difficult to agree with this suggestion in relation to other examples of *perforadores de muleta*, knowing that it was formulated solely on the basis of analysis of photographic material (sic!), of which the originator himself writes.

47. Here, perhaps, it is worth noting that while ineed descriptions and/or sketches of tools called knives are found in the literature (*cuchillos*; i.e.: Lynch 1980, Lavallée 1985; Neira Avendaño 1990), they are rare cases and in the course of bibliographical searches no example was encountered that corresponds to these founds.

48. In other areas, this rock was used almost up to the XX century A.D. for producing projectile points as weapons and tools, and sometimes for knives.

49. Trade exchange, as practiced (even today) by the pastoral people who migrate along the axis of valleys, could remedy this to some extent.

50. Obviously, we must consider the possibility that this raw material was brought by pastoral groups or hunters, whose traces were obliterated by later volcanic activity.

51. The described domes are manifested in the geomorphology of the terrain as steep elevations, prominent peaks, ridges and, here and there, rock walls. They are marked on maps as Cerro Pinta-Cerro Chenje and somewhat further to the south – Cerro Aljajahua. The age of these intrusions is estimated to be the mid- to-late Pliocene, or the same age as the Barroso formation mentioned in this work.

52. Obviously not in a trade sense, but from the biological perspective of energy expenditure *vs* benefit gained (more on this topic in, for example, Aldenderfer 1998).

53. On other terrains, the spread of this raw material is basically linked to the Formative Period (Burger *et al.* 2000), while in the Valley of the Volcanoes is already dominates in the Late/Final Archaic.

54. The sites O.11 and P4 (along with neighboring ones), rich in flakes, should also be analyzed from this same angle.

55. Projectile points of this type are called *corner-notched* in South America. The stem arises from the creation of two notches in the corners of the base of a triangular projectile point.

56. Some of the different proposals for dating should, as said, be rejected due to their exclusively typological and volitional character. Also, certain incongruities in age between typographically similar artifacts from more distant locations can result from differences in cultural development of these terrains.

57. This, after all, further emphasizes the particular role of obsidian on the studied terrain (in this case, especially common), considering that in other areas this material is believed to have been treated as exclusive (Rick 1980) and was used to the smallest flake (Burger *et al.* 2000).

58. Such a situation is described in the valley and on its slopes, as well as at more distant points, including many sites in the *puna* zone.

REFERENCES

Aldenderfer, M. 1998. *Montane Foragers. Asana and South–Central Andean Archaic*. University of Iowa Press, Iowa City, 1–327.

Aldenderfer, M. 2000. Cronologia y conexiones: evidencias preceramicas de Asana. *Boletin de Arqueologia PUCP* 3/1999: 375– 391.

Anovitz, L. M., J. M. Elam, L. R. Riciputi & D. R. Cole. 1999. The failure of obsidian hydration dating: sources, implications, and new directions. *Journal of Archaeological Science* 26: 735–752.

Balaguer, A. 1995. *El valle del fuego/The Valley of Fire*. PANTEL, Lima, 1–191.

Bolin, I. 2002. *Rituals of Respect: The Secret of Survival in the High Peruvian Andes*. University of Texas Press, Austin, 1–311.

Brack, A. 2003. *Perú: diez mil años de domesticación*. Editorial Bruño, Lima, 1–160.

Bruhns, K. O. 1996. *Ancient South America*. Cambridge University Press, Cambridge, 1–424.

Burger, R. L. & F. Asaro. 1977. Analisis de rasgos significativos en la obsidiana de los Andes Centrales. *Revista de Museo Nacional, Lima–Peru* XLIII: 281–325.

Burger, R. L., F. Asaro, P. Trawick & F. Stross. 1998a. The Alca obsidian source: the origin of raw material for Cuzco type obsidian artifacts. *Andean Past* 5: 185–202.

Burger, R. L., F. Asaro, G. Salas & F. Stross. 1998b. The Chivay obsidian source and the geological origin of Titicaca Basin type obsidian artifacts. *Andean Past* 5: 203–223.

Burger, R. L. & M. D. Glascock. 2000a. The Puzolana obsidian source. Locating the geologic source of Ayacucho type obsidian. *Andean Past* 6: 289–307.

Burger, R. L. & M. D. Glascock. 2000b. Locating the Quispisisa obsidian source in the department of Ayacucho, Peru. *Latin American Antiquity* 11(3): 258–268.

Burger, R. L., K. L. Mohr Chávez & S. J. Chávez. 2000. Through the glass darkly: prehispanic obsidian procurement and exchange in Southern Peru and Northern Bolivia. *Journal of World Prehistory* 14(3): 267–362.

Caldas, J. 1993. *Geologia de los cuadrangulos de Huambo y Orcopampa*. Ingemmet, Lima, 1–62.

Cipolla, L. M. 2005. Preceramic period settlement patterns in the Huancané–Putina River Valley, Northern Titicaca Basin, Peru. In: Ch. Stanish, A. B. Cohen & M. Aldenderfer (eds) *Advances in Titicaca Basin Archaeology – 1*. Costen Institute of Archaeology–UCLA, Los Angeles, pp. 55–63.

Deza Rivasplata, J. 1991. *El apogeo de las lanzas – el paleolitico superior andino*. CICA, Lima, 1–122.

Fagan, B. M. 2004. *The Great Journey. The peopling of ancient America*. University Press of Florida, Gainessville, 1–288.

Fiedel, S. J. 1992. *Prehistory of the Americas*. Cambridge University Press, Cambridge, 1–400.

Gałaś, A. & A. Paulo. 2005. Karłowate wulkany formacji Andahua w południowym Peru. *Przegląd Geologiczny* 53(4): 320–326.

Ginter, B. & J. K. Kozłowski. 1990. *Technika obróbki i typologia wyrobów kamiennych paleolitu, mezolitu i neolitu*. PWN, Warszawa, 1–252.

Glascock, M. D. 2006. Complete raport of XRF & NAA obsidian analyses. Unpublished report, Columbia–Missouri, 1–12.

Glascock, M. D., R. J. Speakman & R. L. Burger. 2007. Sources of archaeological obsidian in Peru: description and geochemistry. In: M. D. Glascock, R. J. Speakman & R. S. Popelka-Filcoff (eds) *Archaeological Chemistry: Analytical Techniques and Archaeological Interpretation*. American Chemical Society–Oxford University Press, Washington, pp. 522–552.

Guffroy, J. 1999. *El arte rupestre del Antiguo Perú*. Instituto Frances de Estudios Andinos – Institut de Recherche pour le Devéloppement, Lima, 1–147.

Hanna, J. 2007. *Indian Arrowheads*. Krause Publications, Iola WI, 1–271.

Haury, E. W., E. Antevs & J. F. Lance. 1953. Artifacts with mammoth remains, Naco, Arizona. *American Antiquity* 19(1):

1–24.

Hoempler, A. 1962. Valle de volcanes de Andahua, Arequipa. *Segundo Congreso Nacional de Geologia Societas Geologica, Peru, Lima* 37: 59–69.

Hull, K. L. 2001. Reasserting the utility of obsidian hydration dating: a temperature–dependent empirical approach to practical temporal resolution with archaeological obsidians. *Journal of Archaeological Science* 28: 1025–1040.

Jennings, J. & M. D. Glascock. 2002. Description and method of exploitation of Alca obsidian source, Peru. *Latin American Antiquity* 13(1): 107–118.

Justice, N. D. 1995. *Stone Age Spear and Arrow Points of Midcontinental and Eastern United States.* Indiana University Press, Bloomington–Indianapolis, 1–288.

Kaulicke, P. 1999. Contribuciones hacia la cronologia del Periodo Arcaico en las punas de Junin. *Boletin de Arqueologia PUCP* 3: 307–324.

Klink, C. 2007. The lithic assemblage at Kasapata. In: B.S. Bauer (ed.) *Kasapata and the Archaic Period of the Cuzco Valley.* Costen Institute of Archaeology, Los Angeles, pp.31–77.

Klink, C. & M. Aldenderfer. 2005. A projectile point chronology for the South-Central Andean Highlands. In: Ch. Stanish, A. B. Cohen & M. Aldenderfer (eds) *Advances in Titicaca Basin Archaeology – 1.* Costen Institute of Archaeology–UCLA, Los Angeles, pp.25–54.

Lavallée, D. (ed.). 1985. *Telarmachay – chasseurs et pasteurs préhistoriques des Andes I.* Edition Recherche sur les Civilisations, Paris, 1–461.

Lavallée, D. 2000. *The First South Americans.* The University of Utah Press, Salt Lake City, 1–260.

Linares Málaga, E. 1991–1992. *Prehistoria de Arequipa tomo II.* NN, Arequipa, 1–250.

Lynch, Th. F. (ed.). 1980. *Guitarrero Cave – Early Man in the Andes.* Academic Press, New York, 1–328.

Neira Avendaño, M. 1990. Arequipa Prehispánica. In: M. Neira A., G. Galdos R., A. Malaga M., E. Quiroz P.S. and J.G. Carpio M. (eds) *Historia General de Arequipa.* Fundación M.J. Bustamante De la Fuente–Cuzzi y Cía, Arequipa, pp. 5–184.

Neira Avendaño, M. 1998. Arqueologia de Arequipa. *Cronos – la revista de arqueologia,* 1(1): 9–50.

Olchauski, E. & D. Dávila. 1994. *Geologia de los cuadrangulos de Chuquibamba y Cotahuasi.* Ingemmet, Lima, 1–52.

Paulo, A. 2008. Zarys budowy geologicznej Kordyliery Zachodniej południowego Peru. *Geologia* 34(2/1): 35–53.

Pearsall, D. M. 1980. Pachamachay Ethnobotanical Report: Plant Utilization at a Hunting Base Camp. In: Rick, J. W. *Prehistoric Hunters of the High Andes.* Academic Press, New York, pp.191–231.

Pearsall, D. M. 2003. Plant food resources of the Ecuadorian formative: An overview and comparison to the Central Andes. In: J. S. Raymond & R. L. Burger (eds) *Archaeology of Formative Ecuador.* Dumbarton Oaks, Washington, pp. 213–257.

Perry L., D. H. Sandweiss, D. R. Piperno, K. Rademaker, M. A. Malpass, A. Umire & P. de la Vera. 2006. Early maize agriculture and interzonal interaction in southern Peru. *Nature* 440: 76–79.

Portocarrero, A. 1960. *Reconocimiento geológico del Valle de Andahua.* Tesis de maestro, UNSA Arequipa.

Rick, J. W. 1980. *Prehistoric Hunters of the High Andes.* Academic Press, New York, 1–379.

Rick, J. W. 1996. The character and context of highland preceramic society. In: Keatinge, R. W. (ed.) *Peruvian Prehistory: An Overview of Pre–Inca and Inca Society.* Cambridge University Press, New York, pp. 3–40.

Rogozińska, M. 2008. Tajemnice wierzeń Inków. *National Geographic Polska* 4(103): 22–39.

de Romaña M., J. Blassi & J. Blassi. 1988. *Descubrende el Valle del Colca, el valle perdido de los Incas en Arequipa, Perú.* Mauricio de Romaña y Francis O. Patthey e hijos, Barcelona, 1–204.

Sandweiss, D.H., H. McInnis, R.L. Burger, A. Cano, B. Ojeda, R. Paredes, M. Sandweiss & M. D. Glascock. 1998. Quebrada Jaguay: Early Maritime Adaptations in South America. *Science* 281: 1830–1832.

Schobinger, J. 1988. *Prehistoria de Sudamérica. Culturas precerámicas.* Alianza Editorial, Madrid, 1–490.

Shippee, R. & G. R. Johnson. 1934. A forgotten valley of Peru. *National Geographic Magazine* LXV(1): 111–132.

Squier, E. G. 1870. The primeval monuments of Peru compared with those in other parts of the World. *American Naturalist* 4(1): 1–17.

Stanish, Ch., R. L. Burger, L. M. Cipolla, M. D. Glascock & E. Quelima. 2002. Evidence for early long–distance obsidian exchange and watercraft use from the Southern Lake Titicaca Basin of Bolivia and Peru. *Latin American Antiquity* 13(4): 444–454.

Szykulski, J. 2005. *Pradzieje południowego Peru. Rozwój kulturowy Costa Extremo Sur.* Wyd. Uniwersytetu Wrocławskiego, Wrocław, 1–419.

Wagner, G. A. 1998. *Age Determination of Young Rocks and Artifacts.* Spronger–Verlag, Berlin–Heidelberg–New York, 1–466.

Walanus, A. & T. Goslar. 2004. *Wyznaczanie wieku metodą ^{14}C dla archeologów.* Wyd. Uniwersytetu Rzeszowskiego, Rzeszów, 1–120.

Wasilewski, M. 2005. Udomowienie roślin w Nowym Świecie. *Wiadomości Botaniczne* 49(1/2): 19–37.

Wasilewski, M. 2008. Mineralne leki w Chivay i Dolinie Colca (południowe Peru). *Geologia* 34(2/1): 223–242.

Wasilewski, M. 2009. Algunos medicamentos minerales tradicionales del sur de Perú – su composición y eficacia. *Estudios Latin americanos* 29, (in press).

Ziółkowski, M.S., M.F. Pazdur, A. Krzanowski & A. Michczyński (eds). 1994. *Andes – Radiocarbon Database for Bolivia, Ecuador and Peru.* Andean Archaeological Mission–Gliwice Radiocarbon Laboratory, Warszawa–Gliwice, 1–604.

Ziółkowski, M. S. & L. A. Belan Franco (eds). 2000–2001. Proyecto Arqueológico Condesuyos, Vol.1. *Boletín de la Misión Arqueológica Andina* 3, Warszawa, 1–302.

Ziółkowski, M. S., L. A. Belan Franco & M. Sobczyk (eds). 2005. Proyecto Arqueológico Condesuyos, Vol.2. *Boletín de la Misión Arqueológica Andina* 6, Warszawa, 1–400.

Ziółkowski, M. S., L. A. Belan Franco & M. Sobczyk (eds). 2007. Proyecto Arqueológico Condesuyos, Vol.3. *Boletín de la Misión Arqueológica Andina* 6 – corrected edition, Warszawa, 1–488.

Zwierzęta. Encyklopedia ilustrowana. 2005. PWN, Warszawa, 1–608. Tłum. z angielskiego zespół pod kierownictwem H. Grabarczyka.

Żurowska, K. (ed.). 2001. *Ziołolecznictwo amazońskie i andyjskie.* Tower Press, Gdańsk, 1–319.

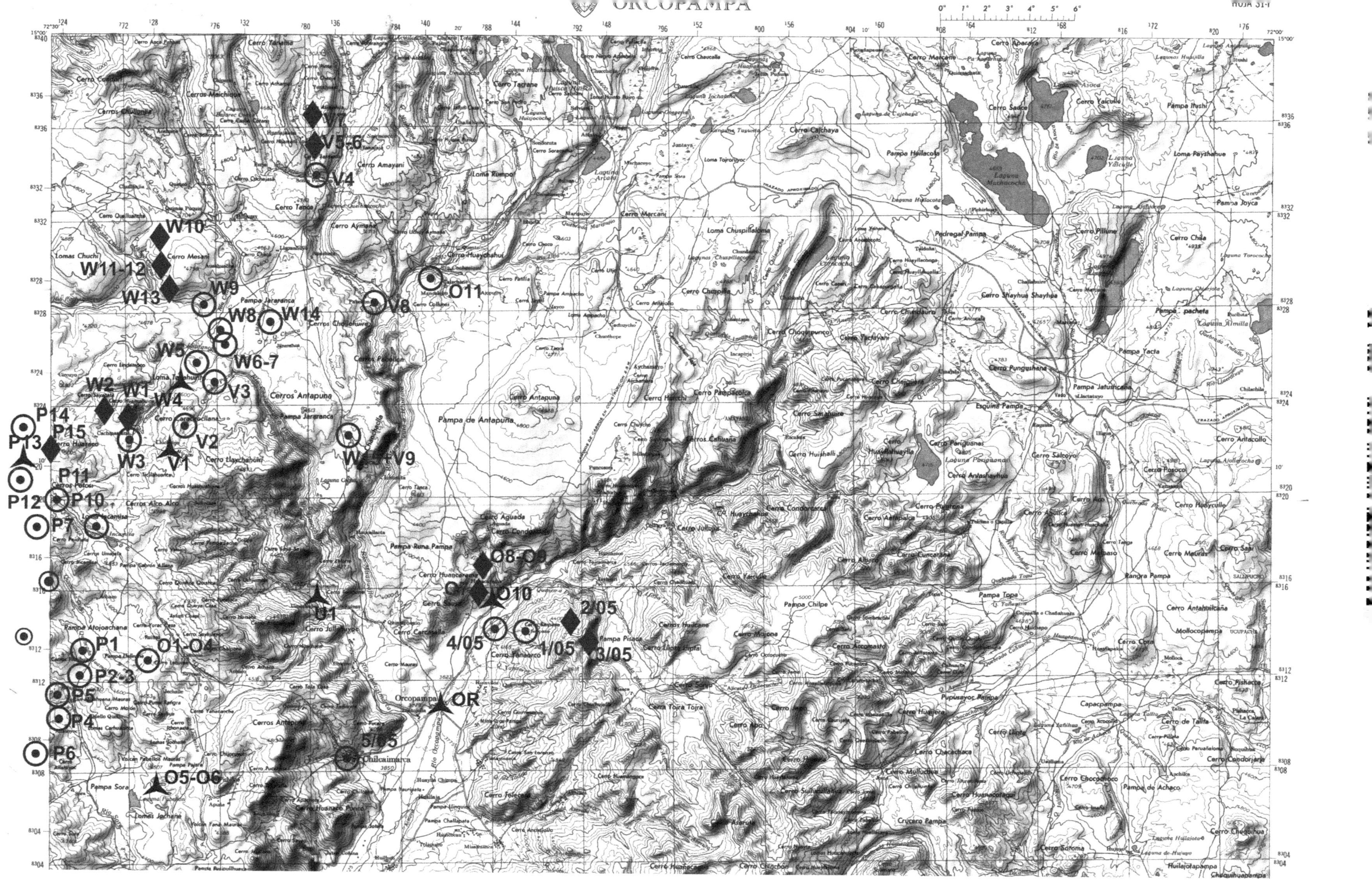
ORCOPAMPA
HOJA 31-T
W7
V5-6
V4
W10
W11-12
W13
W9
W8
W14
W5
W6-7
W2
W1
W4
V3
P14
P15
P13
W3
V2
V1
P11
P12
P10
P7
W15+V9
V8
O11
O8-O9
O10
U1
2/05
1/05
4/05
3/05
O1-O4
P1
P2-3
P5
P4
P6
OR
5/05
O5-O6
Pampa de Antapuna
Cerro Antapuna
Orcopampa
Chilcaimarca
Pampa Jararanca
Cerros Antapuna
Laguna Machucocha
Pampa Chilpe
Pampa Topa
Pampa Pisaca
Pampa Runa Pampa
Pampa Sora

- **archaeological site**
- **outcrop**
- **loose finding**

RGM 1631

PRIMERA EDICION

LEVANTADO POR EL ARMY MAP SERVICE (PV), CUERPO DE INGENIEROS, U.S. ARMY, WASHINGTON, D.C. 1967. POR METODOS FOTOGRAMETRICOS (MULTIPLEX) Y FOTOGRAFIAS AEREAS TOMADAS EN 1955. CONTROL HORIZONTAL Y VERTICAL POR EL IGM EN COLABORACION CON EL AMS. CLASIFICACION DE CAMPO 1962-63.

SIGNOS CONVENCIONALES

En este mapa se consideran que una vía continua en indicios de 2 metros.
El todo rojo representa zonas urbanizadas en las cuales solo se muestran edificios importantes.

CAMINOS
Capital de departamento
Pavimentado, dos o más vías
Afirmado, dos o más vías
Capital de provincia
Transitable en tiempo bueno o seco, de tierra
Capital de distrito
Camino de herradura
Poblados
Sendero
Figurado del terreno
Tunel, Puente
Paso, Puente, Dique o fuerte
Paso, Fuente, Jagüey
Depresión
FERROCARRILES
Trocha normal, una sola vía
Acueducto: Subterráneo, sifonado
Trocha angosta, una sola vía
Estación proyectada
Acueducto: Subterráneo, sifonado
Límite internacional - Alto fronterizo
Zona inundada, Duna, arena seca
Cable transmisor de fuerza eléctrica
Bosque ralo, Bosque espeso
Línea telegráfica
Terreno cultivado, Arrozal
Línea telefónica
Caña de Azúcar, Matorral
Escuela, Iglesia
Río casi una parte del año o quebrada de fondo plano y arenoso
Hacienda, Casa aislada
Cementerio, Cuevas de aterrizaje, Mina
Laguna, Laguna seca una parte del año
Canac, Correo y telégrafo, Correo, telégrafo y teléfono
Río, importante, Pantano
Central de fuerza eléctrica, Telégrafo inalámbrico
Riachuelo, arroyo, quebrada
Horno de fundición, Horno de esparcir ladrillos
Riachuelo, arroyo, quebrada seca una parte del año
Bomba de Agua, Bomba de viento, Pozo de petróleo
Escalonadero, Eras
Tanque, Monumento histórico y ruinas recientes
Quebrada seca, thalweg
Cancha (noráles o alambres)
Canal de irrigación, Estanque
Señal geodésica o altimétrica
Canal de irrigación
Señal geodésica 1º Orden, 2º Orden, Bench Mark
Muelle, Rompeolas
Cota Compañía fotogramétrica

ICA
CHOTA
Costa
Pichncullo

EQUIDISTANCIA 50 METROS CON CURVAS SUPLEMENTARIAS CADA 25 METROS
COTAS REFERIDAS AL NIVEL MEDIO DEL MAR

PROYECCION TRANSVERSAL MERCATOR
DATUM HORIZONTAL PROVISIONAL DE SUR AMERICA

Escala 1:100,000

CUADRICULA TRANSVERSAL MERCATOR CADA 4 KILOMETROS ZONA 18
ESFEROIDE INTERNACIONAL
LOS TRAZOS Y NUMEROS EN SEPIA EN LA LINEA MARGINAL CORRESPONDEN
A LA CUADRICULA TRANSVERSAL MERCATOR DE LA ZONA 19

AREA LEVANTADA 2,975.39 Km²

REIMPRESO EN EL INSTITUTO GEOGRAFICO MILITAR LIMA-PERU 1977

ABREVIATURAS

Acueducto	Acu	Isla	I.ª
Bomba	B.ª	Laguna	L.ª
Canal de irrigación	C.I	Nevado	Nev.ª
Cerro	C.º	Pampa	Pp.ª
Embarcadero	Emb.º	Punta	Pt.ª
Estación	Est.ª	Quebrada	Q.
Estanque	E.que	Señal Geodésica	Sa.ª
Fábrica	F.ª	Urbanización	Urb.
Hacienda	H.da	Volcán	V.

DECLINACION MAGNETICA APROXIMADA EN 1977
PARA TODA LA HOJA
VARIA ANUALMENTE Fº 3 OESTE

ORCOPAMPA — DEPARTAMENTO DE AREQUIPA — PERU

www.ingramcontent.com/pod-product-compliance
Lightning Source LLC
Chambersburg PA
CBHW051309270326
41929CB00029B/3466